SOLOMON MAIMON

AN AUTOBIOGRAPHY

Edited and with an Epilogue by Moses Hadas

SCHOCKEN BOOKS / NEW YORK

Manufactured in the U.S.A. by H Wolff, New York

CONTENTS

SOLOMON MAIMON

CHAPTER I

Grandfather's Ménage

MY GRANDFATHER, HEIMANN JOSEPH, HELD THE LEASE of certain villages in the estates of Prince Radzivil, in the neighborhood of the town of Mir. For his own residence he chose one of these villages, Sukoviborg by name, which lay on the river Niemen. Here, besides a few peasants' plots, there were a water mill, a landing stage, and a warehouse for the vessels which plied from Koenigsberg in Prussia. These appurtenances, together with a bridge back of the village and, on the other side, a drawbridge on the Niemen, belonged to the leasehold, which was then valued at about a thousand gulden and constituted grandfather's *hazakah*.[1] The warehouse and the river traffic made the leasehold lucrative. With industry and good management, *si mens non laeva fuisset,* grandfather should have been able not only to maintain his household but to accumulate wealth. But the inefficient organization of the country and his own lack of even rudimentary knowledge of the economic utilization of land put great obstacles in his way.

Traffic was heavy and the bridges in bad repair, so that it not infrequently happened that they broke down just as some Polish nobleman with his rich entourage was passing, and horse and rider would be plunged into the swamp. The wretched leaseholder was then dragged to the bridge, where he was laid down and flogged till the demands of vengeance seemed satisfied. Grandfather did all he could to pre-

[1] *Hazakah* is the right of possession, which, according to Jewish law, assured a holder permanent tenure after three years of continuous occupancy. In parts of Europe (as in Italy, where it was called *ius gazaga*) this usage was recognized by secular courts.

3

vent repetition of such inconvenience. To this end he posted one of his people to keep constant watch at the bridge, so that if any noble should pass and the expected accident befall, the sentinel might bring word to the house with all speed and the family thus have time to take refuge in the nearby wood. Upon such occasions everyone would run out of the house in terror, and it sometimes happened that all were constrained to pass the night without a roof, until one and then another ventured to approach the house.

One such incident took place when I was a child of three. Everyone ran out of the house, among them the maid, with me in her arms. But the servants of the passing nobleman ran in pursuit, and so she quickened her pace and in her haste let me fall from her arms. There I lay whimpering at the edge of the wood, until a peasant chanced to pass, who lifted me up and carried me to his house. Only after quiet was restored and the family was returned to the house did the maid recollect that she had lost me in her flight, whereupon she commenced to wail and wring her hands. They sought me everywhere but could not find me, until at length the peasant came from the village and restored me to my parents.

In his own environment my grandfather was esteemed a rich man, which he might indeed have been if he had understood how to exploit his opportunities. But his reputation for wealth brought him the envy and hatred of all, even of his own family. The landlord neglected him, his steward found diverse means of oppressing him, and his own domestics and strangers alike cheated and robbed him. In a word, he was the poorest rich man in the world.

Other and greater misfortunes, of which I feel constrained to make mention, afflicted him. The Papa, which is to say the Russian cleric in the village, was a stupid and ignorant clod, barely able to read and write. Most of his time he spent at the tavern, drinking with his boorish parishioners, and he always had his liquor charged to his account, with never a thought of paying his score. Grandfather at last wearied of this, and determined to extend no further credit. As was to be expected, the man took umbrage, and meditated vengeance.

Eventually he hit upon a device, frightful indeed in the eyes of humanity, but one of which Catholic Christians in the Poland of the period were wont to make frequent use. His scheme was to charge my grandfather with the murder of a Christian, and so compass his death by judicial hanging. The circumstances were as follows. A beaver trapper who haunted the region for the game which was to be taken on the Niemen sometimes sold his catch to my grandfather; this had to be done secretly, for beavers are a royal preserve, and all that are taken must be delivered to the court. Once the trapper came about midnight, knocked, and had grandfather summoned. He displayed a bag, quite heavy to lift, and said with a mysterious air: "I have brought you a stout fellow here." Grandfather wished to strike a light, examine the beaver, and dicker for it with the trapper. But the trapper said there was no need: grandfather could take the beaver, and they would be sure to agree upon terms afterwards. Grandfather suspected no evil, and so took the sack just as it was, laid it aside, and again betook himself to rest. But he had scarcely fallen asleep when he was again aroused by loud knocking.

It was the priest, with some boors from the village, who at once began to make a thorough search of the house. They found the sack, and grandfather was terrified, though he could suspect no worse than that he had been informed against on account of his clandestine traffic in beavers and would not be in position to protest innocence. But how great was his horror when the sack was opened and instead of a beaver a human corpse came to view!

Straightway grandfather's hands were bound behind his back, his feet were put into stocks, he was cast into a cart, brought to the town of Mir, and there delivered to the criminal court. He was made fast in fetters and thrust into a dungeon. At the trial my grandfather insisted upon his innocence, related the events exactly as they had transpired, and, reasonably enough, demanded that the trapper too should be examined. But the trapper was nowhere to be found; he was already over the hills and far away. Search was instituted, but the bloodthirsty judge found the delay tedious, and thrice running ordered grandfather subjected to torture. Grandfather persisted in his asseveration of his innocence of murder.

At last the hero of the beavers was discovered. He was examined, and as he denied the whole affair straightway, he too was subjected to trial by torture, whereupon his story tumbled forth. He declared that he had found the dead body in the water some time previously, and had wished to fetch it to the parsonage for burial. But the priest had said to him: "There is time enough for burial. You know that the Jews are a stubborn people, and hence damned to all eternity. They have crucified our Lord Jesus Christ, and to this day they seek Christian blood, if they can manage to obtain any, for use at their paschal festival, which they have instituted as a mark of their triumph. They use the blood for their Passover loaves. You will be performing a meritorious deed if you can smuggle this dead body into the house of that accursed Jew of a leaseholder. You will of course have to clear out, but then your trade you can drive anywhere." Upon this confession the fellow was whipped and my grandfather set free; but the priest continued priest.

For an everlasting memorial of this, my grandfather's deliverance from death, my father composed in Hebrew a sort of epic poem interspersed with songs, in which the narrative of the whole event is related and God's goodness celebrated. The rule was established that the day of deliverance should be celebrated in the family annually, and that at this celebration the poem should be recited, just as the Book of Esther is read at the Purim festival.

Prince Radzivil, who was a great lover of the chase, came one day with his whole court to hunt in the neighborhood of our village. Among the party was his daughter who afterwards married Prince Rawuzki. The young princess, in order to enjoy rest at noon, betook herself with the ladies of her court, the servants-in-waiting, and the lackeys, to the very room, where as a boy I was sitting behind the stove. I was struck with astonishment at the magnificence and splendor of the court, gazed with rapture at the beauty of the persons and at the dresses with their trimmings of gold and silver lace; I could not satisfy my eyes with the sight. My father came just as I was beside myself with joy, and had broken into the words, "Oh, how beautiful!" In order to calm me, and at the same time to confirm me in the principles of our faith, he whispered into my ear, "Little fool, in the other world the *duksel* will kindle the *pezsure* for us," which means, In the future life the princess will kindle the stove for us. No one can conceive the sort of feeling this statement produced in me. On the one hand, I believed my

7

father, and was very glad about this future happiness in store for us; but at the same time I felt pity for the poor princess who was going to be doomed to such a degrading service. On the other hand, I could not get it into my head that this beautiful rich princess in this splendid dress should ever make a fire for a poor Jew. I was thrown into the greatest perplexity on the subject, till some game drove these thoughts out of my head.

CHAPTER II

Early Reminiscences—Education Formal and Informal

HERE I MUST RELATE ONE ANECDOTE, BECAUSE IT IS THE earliest recollection of my childhood. I was about three years old at the time. There were always merchants put up at our place, and especially *shoffers*, that is to say, gentlemen who undertook the purchase and delivery of goods on behalf of the great nobles. These people were extremely fond of me because of my liveliness, and played all manner of pranks with me. Because of her slight figure and her lively nature these jolly gentlemen bestowed upon my mother the nickname Kuza, which signifies young filly. Since I heard them often call my mother Kuza and had no knowledge of the word's meaning, I also came to call her Mama Kuza. She forbade me to do so, and said: "God punishes anyone who calls his mother Mama Kuza." One of these *shoffers*, Piliezki by name, used to take tea at our house daily, and would entice me to his side by offering me a bit of sugar. One morning while he was drinking his tea and I had placed myself in the customary position for receiving my sugar, he said he would give it to me only if I should say Mama Kuza.

As my mother was present I refused to do so. He motioned my mother to go into an adjoining room. As soon as she had shut the door I went to him and whispered Mama Kuza in his ear. But he insisted that I pronounce the words aloud, and promised he would give me a piece of sugar as often as I pronounced the words aloud. Thereupon I said: "Mr. Piliezki wishes me to say Mama Kuza, but I will not say Mama Kuza, for God punishes anyone who says Mama Kuza." I got my three pieces of sugar.

From childhood on I had inclination and skill for drawing. In my father's house, to be sure, I never had opportunity to see a product of the draftsman's art, but I did find woodcuts of foliage, birds, and the like on the title pages of certain Hebrew books. These woodcuts afforded me great pleasure, and I sought to copy them with a bit of chalk or charcoal. The thing that contributed most to my inclination was a Hebrew book of fables, in which the dramatis personae, naturally animals, were represented by woodcuts. I copied all the figures with the utmost faithfulness. My father admired my skill but at the same time rebuked me, saying: "Do you wish to become a painter? You must study Talmud and become a rabbi. Whoso understands the Talmud understands all."

In his study my father had a cupboard filled with books, but he forbade me to read any but the Talmud. But prohibitions were of no avail. Since household affairs occupied most of my father's time, I took advantage of the opportunities his preoccupation afforded. Curiosity drove me to the cupboard, and I leafed through all the books. I possessed a fair command of Hebrew, and found that more pleasure was to be found in some of these books than in the Talmud.

9

The most valuable books in the collection were the following. There was a Hebrew chronicle entitled *Zemah David,* composed by a sensible chief rabbi in Prague called David Gans. Gans was also the author of the astronomical book to be mentioned presently; he had enjoyed the distinction of acquaintance with Tycho Brahe and had made astronomical observations with Brahe in the Copenhagen Observatory. There were, besides, a Josephus, evidently garbled, and a history of the persecutions of the Jews in Spain and Portugal. But what attracted me most powerfully was the astronomical work. Here a new world was laid open before me, and I gave myself to it with the greatest diligence. Think of a child of about seven, situated as I was, with an astronomical work thrown in his way and exciting his interest. I had no notion of the first elements of mathematics. There was no one to give me guidance, for, needless to say, I dared not let my curiosity even be known to my father, nor, even if he would, could he have enlightened me. How must the spirit of a child, thirsting for knowledge, have been inflamed by such a discovery! This the result will show.

As I was still a child, and the beds in my father's house were few, I was allowed to sleep with my old grandmother, whose bed stood in the above-mentioned study. As I was obliged during the day to occupy myself solely with the study of the Talmud, and durst not take another book in my hand, I devoted the evenings to my astronomical inquiries. Accordingly after my grandmother had gone to bed, I put fresh wood on the fire, made for the cupboard, and took out my beloved astronomical book. My grandmother indeed scolded me, because it was too cold for the old lady to lie alone in bed; but I did not trouble myself about that, and continued my study till the fire was burnt out.

After I had carried this on for some evenings, I came to the description of the celestial sphere and its imaginary circles, designed for the explanation of astronomical phenomena. This was represented in the book by a single figure, in connection with which the author gave the reader the good advice, that, since the manifold circles could not be represented in a plane figure except by straight lines, he should, for the sake of rendering them more clearly intelligible, make for himself either an ordinary globe or an armillary sphere. I therefore resolved to make such a sphere out of twisted rods; and after I had finished this work, I was in a position to understand the whole book. But as I had to take care lest my father should find out how I had been occupied, I always hid my armillary sphere in a corner behind the cupboard before I went to bed.

CHAPTER III

Jewish Schools and the Joy of Release from Them

MY BROTHER JOSEPH AND I WERE SENT TO MIR TO school. My brother, who was about twelve years old, was put to board with a schoolmaster of some repute at that time, Yossel by name. This man was the terror of all young people, the scourge of God. He treated his charges with incredible cruelty, flogged them till the blood came, even for the slightest offense, and not infrequently tore off their ears, or beat their eyes out. When the parents of these unfortunates came to him, and brought him to task, he struck them with stones or whatever else came to hand, and drove them with his stick out of the house back to their own dwellings, with no respect of persons. All under his discipline became either blockheads or good scholars. I was only seven years old at the time and was sent to another schoolmaster.

I must now say something of the condition of the Jewish schools in general. The school is commonly a small, smoky hut, and the children are scattered, some on benches, some on the bare earth. The master, in a dirty blouse, sits on the table and holds between his knees a bowl in which he grinds tobacco into snuff with a huge pestle like the club of Hercules, while at the same time he wields his authority. The ushers give lessons, each in his own corner, and rule those under their charge quite as despotically as the master himself. Of the breakfast, lunch, and other food sent to the school for the children, these gentlemen keep the largest share for themselves. Sometimes the poor youngsters get nothing at all; and yet they dare not complain on pain of incurring the vengeance of these tyrants. Here the children are imprisoned from morning to night, and have not an hour to themselves, except only an afternoon on Fridays and at the New Moon.

As the children are doomed in the bloom of youth to such an inferno of a school, it may be easily imagined with what joy and rapture they look forward to their release.

CHAPTER IV

My Family Reduced to Misery

MY FATHER HAD ONCE SHIPPED IN A VESSEL OF PRINCE Radzivil's some barrels of salt and herrings which he had bought in Koenigsberg. When he came home and was going to fetch his goods, the agent, Schachna, absolutely refused to let him take them. My father then showed the bill of lading, which he had got on the shipment of the goods; but the agent tore it out of his hands, and threw it into the fire. My father thus found himself compelled to carry on a long and costly suit, which he must needs postpone till the following year, when he would again make the journey to Koenigsberg. Here he obtained a certificate from the customhouse, showing that he had shipped the said goods in a vessel of Prince Radzivil's under the direction of Herr Schachna. On this certificate the agent was summoned before the court, but found it convenient not to make an appearance; and my father gained the suit in the first, second, and third instances. In spite of this, however, as a consequence of the wretched administration of justice in Poland at the time, my father had no power to execute this decision, and though his suit was successful he was not even able to recover the costs.

To this was added the further result, that by his suit he had made of Herr Schachna an enemy who now persecuted him in every possible way. This the cunning scoundrel could accomplish very well, as by all sorts of intrigues he had been appointed by Prince Radzivil steward of all his estates situated in the district of Mir. He resolved therefore on my father's ruin, and only waited for a convenient opportunity to carry out his revenge.

This he found soon; and indeed a Jew, who was named after his farm Schwersen, and was known as the biggest scoundrel in the whole district, offered him a hand. This fellow was an ignoramus, did not even understand the Jewish language, and therefore used Russian. He occupied himself mainly in keeping an eye on the farms in the neighborhood, and he knew how to get possession of the most lucrative among them by offering a higher rent and bribing the steward. Without troubling himself in the least about the law of the *Hazakah*, he drove the old legal farmers from their possessions, and by this means enriched himself. Thus he lived in wealthy and prosperous circumstances, and in this state reached an advanced age.

The scoundrel had long had his eye on my grandfather's farm, and merely waited for a favorable opportunity and a plausible pretext to get possession of it for himself. Unfortunately my granduncle Jacob, who lived in another village belonging to my grandfather's leasehold, had fallen into debt to Schwersen to the amount of some fifty-six dollars. As he could not meet his obligation when it fell due, his creditor came with certain servants of the manor, and threatened to seize the cauldron, which constituted my granduncle's whole wealth. In consternation he secretly loaded the cauldron upon a wagon, drove with all haste to my grandfather's, and, without letting any of us know, hid the vessel in the marsh which lay behind our house. But his creditor followed on his heels and came to my grandfather's. They made thorough search, but could find the cauldron nowhere. Irritated at his failure and breathing vengeance against my grandfather who, he believed, had prevented his success, he rode to the town, carried an imposing present to the steward, and offered double the rent for my grandfather's leasehold, besides an annual voluntary gift for the steward.

This gentleman was overjoyed by the offer, and mindful of the disgrace which my father, a Jew, had brought upon him, a Polish noble, by the suit mentioned above, he concluded on the spot a contract with the scoundrel, by which he not only gave over to him the leasehold, with all the rights pertaining to it, even before the end of my grandfather's term, but also robbed my grandfather of all he had—barns full of grain, cattle, and the like—and shared the plunder with the new tenant.

My grandfather was therefore obliged to quit his dwelling-place in mid-winter with his whole family, and, without knowing where he should settle again, to wander about from place to place. Our departure from this place was very affecting. The whole neighborhood lamented our fate.

CHAPTER V

New Abode, New Misery—The Talmudist

AND SO WE WANDERED ABOUT THE COUNTRYSIDE LIKE the Israelites in the wilderness of Arabia, without knowing where or when we should find a resting place. At last we came to a village which belonged to two landlords. The one part was already leased; but the landlord of the other could not lease his, because he had still to build a house. Weary of wandering about in winter with a whole family, my grandfather resolved to take a lease of this house, which was still to be built, along with its appurtenances, and meanwhile, till the house was ready, to make shift as well as he could. Accordingly we were obliged to take up our quarters in a barn. The other farmer did all in his power to prevent our settlement in the place; but to no avail. The building was finished, we took possession, and began to keep house. But unfortunately everything went awry; nothing would succeed.

Immediately after this I was sent to school at Iwenez,

about fifteen miles distant, and here I began to study the Talmud. The study of the Talmud is the chief object of higher education among our people. Riches, bodily advantages, and talents of every kind have indeed a certain worth in their eyes and are esteemed in proportion; but among them no merit is superior to that of a good Talmudist. He has the first claim upon all offices and positions of honor in the community. If he enters an assembly, whatever his age or rank, every one rises before him out of respect, and the most honorable place is assigned to him. He is director of ordinary men's conscience, their lawgiver, and their judge. One who does not show such a scholar proper respect is, according to the judgment of the Talmudists, damned to all eternity. The common man dare not enter upon the most trivial undertaking, if, in the judgment of the scholar, it is not according to law. Religious usages, allowed and forbidden meats, marriage and divorce are determined not only by the enormous accumulated mass of rabbinical law, but also by special rabbinical judgments which deduce special cases from the general laws. A wealthy merchant, leaseholder or professional man with a marriageable daughter, does everything in his power to acquire a good Talmudist as son-in-law. In other respects the scholar may be deformed, diseased, and ignorant: he will still have the advantage over rivals. At the betrothal the future father-in-law of such a phoenix is obliged to pay to the parents of the youth a sum fixed by previous agreement; and besides the dowry for his daughter, he is further obliged to provide her and her husband with food, clothing, and lodging, for six or eight years after their marriage, during which time the interest on the dowry is paid, so that the learned son-in-law may continue his studies at his father-in-law's expense. After this period he receives the dowry in hand, and then he is either promoted to some learned office, or he spends his whole life in learned leisure. In either case the wife undertakes the management of the household and the conduct of business; and she is content if only in return for all her toils she becomes in some measure a partaker of her husband's fame and future blessedness.

CHAPTER VI

"Joy Endureth But a Little"

I HAVE SAID THAT I WAS SENT TO SCHOOL AT IWENEZ. My father gave me a letter to the chief rabbi of this place, who was a relation of ours, requesting him to give me in charge to an able teacher, and to exercise surveillance over the progress of my studies. But the rabbi gave me in charge to a common schoolmaster, and told me I was to visit him every Sabbath so that he might examine me himself. This injunction I followed punctually; but the arrangement did not continue long. At one of these examinations I began to dispute about my lessons and to suggest difficulties. Without replying to them, the chief rabbi asked me if I had stated these difficulties to my teacher also.

"Of course," I replied.

"And what did he say?" asked the chief rabbi.

"Nothing to the point," I replied, "except that he enjoined silence on me, and said, 'A youngster must not be too inquisitive; he must see to it merely that he understands his lesson, and not overwhelm his teacher with questions.'"

"Ah!" said the chief rabbi, "your teacher is altogether too easygoing, we must make a change. I will give you instruction myself. I will do it merely out of friendship, and I hope that your father will have as little objection as your former teacher. The fee which your father pays for your education will be given to your teacher with no deduction."

And so the chief rabbi became my teacher. He struck out upon a path of his own. There were no weekly lessons to be repeated till impressed on the memory, no tasks for the pupil to perform, in which the course of his thoughts is very often arrested for the sake of a single word or expression which has little to do with the main subject. My teacher's method was very different. He had me explain something from the Talmud *ex tempore* in his presence, conversed with me on the subject, explained to me as much as was necessary to set my own mind in motion, and by means of questions and answers turned my attention away from all side issues to the main subject. The result was that I quickly passed through all three stages in the study of the Talmud.

My father, to whom the chief rabbi gave an account of his plan and of my progress, was beside himself with joy. He rendered his warmest thanks to this excellent man for taking such pains with me out of mere friendship, and that notwithstanding his delicate state of health, for he was consumptive. But this joy did not long endure; before half a year the chief rabbi was called to his fathers, and I was left like a sheep without a shepherd.

The news was brought to my father, who came and fetched me home. Not, however, to H...., from which I had been sent to school, but to Mohilna, about six miles from H...., whither my father had meanwhile removed.

CHAPTER VII

The Ungodly Provideth, and the Righteous Putteth It On"

HERE IS AN INCIDENT WHICH HAPPENED TO ME AND HAD
a comical sequel. The Russians had been quartered for
some time in Mohilna, and when they were issued new
mountings for their uniforms they were allowed to
sell the old. My eldest brother Joseph and my cousin
Beer applied to Russian acquaintances of theirs, and
received some brass buttons as a present. They regarded these buttons an elegant decoration, and had
them sewn on their hose instead of the wooden buttons
they had previously worn. I too was taken with the
baubles, but as I wanted skill to provide myself by
my own diligence, I was constrained to use compul-
sion. I applied to my father, and demanded that
Joseph and Beer be required to share their buttons
with me. My father was extremely fair, yet cherished
me above all else. He said that the buttons were, to be
sure, the rightful property of their owners, but inasmuch as these owners had more than they required for
their own wants, it was but just that they should give
me some of the excess. To commend me and shame
them he added a verse of Scripture: "The ungodly
provideth, and the righteous putteth it on." This decision must needs be carried out despite the protest of
Joseph and Beer; and I too could preen myself with
shining brass buttons on my hose.

But Joseph and Beer could not stomach their loss.
They complained loudly of the impious wrong which
had been done them. My father, wishing to be rid of
the suit told them that, as the buttons had been already
sewn on Solomon's hose, they must not use force, but
that if they could recover them by stratagem, they
were at liberty to do so. Both were pleased with this

decision. They came to me, looked at my buttons and together exclaimed in astonishment, "Oh! what is that we see? Buttons sewn on cloth hose with linen instead of hemp thread! They must come off at once." While they were speaking, they removed all the buttons, and went off rejoicing over their successful stratagem. I ran after them, and demanded that they should sew the buttons on again; but they laughed me to scorn. My father said to me, smiling: "Since you are so credulous and allow yourself to be duped, I can no longer help you. I hope you will be wiser in the future." With this the suit was concluded. I was obliged to content myself with wooden buttons, and to hear Joseph and Beer often repeat to my mortification the biblical passage which my father had used to my advantage: "The ungodly provideth, and the righteous putteth it on."

CHAPTER VIII

Love Affairs and Matrimonial Proposals

IN MY YOUTH I WAS VERY LIVELY, AND MY NATURE HAD much that was agreeable. In my passions I was violent and impatient. Till about my eleventh year, as my upbringing was very strict and I was kept from all contact with women, I felt no special inclination towards the fair sex. But an incident produced a great change in me in this respect.

A poor but very pretty girl about my own age was taken into our house as a servant. She charmed me uncommonly. Desires began to stir in me, which I had previously never known. But in accordance with the strict rabbinical morality, I was obliged to guard against casting an attentive eye on the girl, and still more against speaking with her; only now and then was I able to throw a stolen glance.

Our landlord neighbor had two sons and three daughters. The eldest daughter, Deborah, was already married. The second, Pessel, was about my age; the local peasantry professed to find a certain resemblance in our features, and therefore conjectured that by all the laws of probability there would be a match between us. We two also had an inclination towards one another. But by ill luck the youngest daughter, Rachel, fell down a cellar and dislocated a leg. The girl recovered completely, but her leg remained somewhat crooked. The landlord then started a hunt after me; he was altogether determined to have me for son-in-law. My father was quite agreeable to the relationship but wished to have as his daughter-in-law the straight-legged Pessel rather than Rachel of the crooked leg. The landlord, however, declared that this was impossible, inasmuch as he had fixed on a rich husband for the elder, while the younger was destined for me; and as my father was unable to give me anything, he was willing to provide for her richly out of his own fortune. Besides a considerable sum which he agreed to give as a portion, he was willing in addition to make me joint heir of his fortune, and to provide me with all necessaries the whole of my life. Moreover, he promised to pay my father a fixed sum immediately after the betrothal, and not only to leave him undisturbed in his rights, but also to seek to promote his domestic prosperity in every way possible.

Had my father heeded these representations, he would without doubt have established the fortune of his house, and I should have lived with a spouse, who, it is true, had a crooked leg, but (as I found out some time afterwards when I was tutor in her family) was in other respects an amiable woman. I should thus have been freed from all cares and in the lap of fortune, and I should have been able to apply myself to my studies without hindrance. But unhappily my father scorned this proposal. He was absolutely determined to have Pessel for his daughter-in-law; and since this was impossible, the two families began to feud. But as the landlord was rich and my father poor, he naturally drew the short end of the stick.

Some time afterwards another matrimonial proposal for me turned up. Mr. L.... of Schmilowitz, a learned and at the same time a rich man, who had an only daughter, was so enchanted with my fame, that he chose me for his son-in-law without having set eyes upon me. He began by entering into correspondence with my father on the subject, and left it to him to stipulate the conditions. My father answered his letter in lofty style, compounded of biblical verses and passages from the Talmud, in which he expressed the conditions briefly by means of the following verse from the Canticles (8:12): "Thou, O Solomon, shalt have the thousand, and those that keep the fruit thereof two hundred." Consent was given on all points.

My father accordingly journeyed to Schmilowitz, saw his future daughter-in-law, and had the marriage contract drawn in accordance with the terms agreed upon. Two hundred gulden were paid to him on the spot. He was not content with this sum, however, but insisted that in his letter he had been obliged to limit himself to two hundred gulden merely for the sake of the beautiful verse which he did not wish to spoil: he would not enter into the transaction at all unless he received for himself twice two hundred gulden (fifty thalers in Polish money). They had therefore to pay him two hundred gulden more, and to hand over to him the "little presents" for me, namely, a cap of black velvet trimmed with gold lace, a Bible bound in green velvet with silver clasps, and similar gifts. With these things he came home rejoicing, gave me the presents, and told me that I was to prepare myself for a disputation to be held on my marriage day, which would fall two months hence.

Already my mother had begun to bake the cakes she was expected to take with her to the wedding, and to prepare all manner of preserves; and I began to think about the disputation I was to hold, when suddenly the mournful news arrived that my bride had died of smallpox. My father could easily reconcile himself to this loss, by reflecting that he had made fifty thalers by his son in an honorable way, and might now receive another fifty thalers for him. Neither could I, never having seen my bride, particularly mourn her loss; I thought to myself, "The cap and the silver-clasped Bible are already mine, and a bride will also not be long awanting; as for my disputation, it can serve me another time." My mother alone was disconsolate over the loss. Cakes and preserves are of a perishable nature and will not keep long. The labor which my mother had expended was therefore rendered fruitless by the fatal mishap. Furthermore, she could find no safe place to keep the delicacies from my secret attacks.

CHAPTER IX

I Become an Object of Contention, Get Two Wives at Once, and Am at Last Kidnapped

MEANWHILE THE DOMESTIC CIRCUMSTANCES OF MY father deteriorated daily. He found himself compelled to journey to the town of Nesvij, a provincial capital, there to seek employment as teacher, and I too must needs follow. Here, under favorable conditions, he opened a school of his own, in which he could employ me as assistant.

A widow, celebrated for her superior talents as well as for her Xanthippe-like character, kept a tavern at the extremity of one of the suburbs. She had a daughter inferior to herself in no particular and indispensable in the management of the house. Madam Rissia (for such was the widow's name), aroused by my constantly increasing reputation, fixed on me as a husband for her daughter Sarah. Her family represented to her the impossibility of executing her design: first, my father's pride, and the demands which he would therefore make, and which she could never satisfy; then my fame, which had already provoked the attention of the most prominent and wealthy people of the town; and finally, the moderate character of her own fortune, which was far from sufficient to carry out such a proposal. Such representations, however, moved her not at all. She had once for all taken it into her head to have me for a son-in-law, cost what it might; and she thought the devil would needs be in it if she could not get the young man of her choice.

She sent a proposal to my father, gave him no rest all the time he was in the town, discussed the matter with him herself on sundry occasions, and promised to satisfy all his demands. My father sought to gain time for deliberation, and to let the matter drag. But the time came when we were to return home. My father went with me to the widow's house, which was the last on our road, there to wait for a conveyance which started from that point. Madam Rissia made use of the opportunity, began to caress me, introduced my bride, and asked me how I was pleased with her.

At last she pressed for a decisive answer from my father. He continued to hold back, however, and sought in every way possible to represent the difficulties involved.

While they were thus treating with one another, suddenly there burst into the room the chief rabbi, the preacher, and the elders of the place, along with many of the local worthies. This sudden apparition was achieved without magic. These gentlemen had been invited to a circumcision at the house of a prominent man in this very suburb. Madam Rissia, who knew this very well, at once sent her son to the house with an invitation to the whole company to adjourn, immediately upon rising from table, to a betrothal at her house. And so they came half intoxicated; and as they believed nothing else than that all the preliminaries of the marriage contract had been settled, and that nothing was wanting but to write out and subscribe the document, they sat down to table and set my father in their midst; and the chief rabbi began to dictate the contract to the scribe of the community.

My father assured them that on the main point nothing had as yet been decided, and that still less had the preliminary articles been settled. Thereupon the chief rabbi fell into a passion, for he supposed that it was only a quibble, and that his sacred person and the whole honorable company were being made sport of. He turned to the company with a haughty air and said: "Who is this Rabbi Joshua, who makes himself of so much consequence?" My father replied: "The Rabbi is superfluous. I am, 'tis true, but a common man; yet I believe no one can dispute my right to care for the welfare of my son, and to place his future happiness on a firm footing."

The chief rabbi was greatly offended with the ambiguity of the expression, "The Rabbi is superfluous." He realized that he had no right to lay down laws to my father in the matter, and that Madam Rissia was precipitate in inviting a company to a betrothal before the parties were agreed on the preliminary articles. He therefore struck a humbler tone. He represented to my father the advantages of this match, the high ancestry of the bride (her grandfather, father, and uncle having been learned men, and chief rabbis), her personal attractions, and the willingness and ability of Madam Rissia to satisfy all his demands.

My father, who in fact could refute nothing of all this, was compelled to yield. The marriage contract was drawn up, and in it Madam Rissia made over to her daughter her tavern with all that pertained to it as a bridal portion, and in addition undertook an obligation to board and clothe the newly-married couple for six years. Besides, I received as a present the entire Talmud with its appurtenances, together worth two or three hundred thalers, and a number of other gifts. My father assumed no obligation at all, and in addition received fifty thalers in cash. Very prudently he had refused to accept a bill for this sum but demanded payment before the betrothal.

After all this had been arranged, there was a capital entertainment, and the brandy flask was vigorously plied. The very next day my father and I went home. My mother-in-law promised to send after us as soon as possible the "little presents" and the articles of clothing for me which she had not been able to get ready for the hasty departure. But many weeks passed without our hearing or seeing anything of these articles. My father was perplexed, and as the character of my mother-in-law had long been suspect to him, he could think no other than that the intriguing woman was seeking some subterfuge to escape from her burdensome obligation. Hence he resolved to repay like with like.

He was confirmed in his resolution by the following circumstance. A rich landlord who used to bring spirits to Nesvij for sale and to lodge in our house on his journey through Mohilna, had likewise cast his eye upon me. He had an only daughter, and he privately fixed on me as a husband for her. He knew, however, what difficulties would confront him, if he were to treat directly with my father. He therefore chose an indirect approach. His plan was to make my father his debtor; and as father's pinched circumstances would make it impossible for him to meet the debt, he expected to force him, as it were, to consent to this union as a means of erasing his indebtedness in consideration of the sum stipulated for his son. Accordingly he offered my father sundry kegs of spirits on credit, and the offer was accepted with alacrity.

As the date of payment approached, Hersch Dukor (such was the landlord's name) came to dun my father. Father told him that he was not at the moment in position to meet the debt, and begged him to have patience for yet a while. "Herr Joshua," said the landlord, "I will speak with you quite frankly on this matter. Your circumstances are growing daily worse; and if no fortunate accident intervenes, I do not see any possibility of your being able to clear off your debt. The best thing for us both, therefore, is this. You have a son, and I have a daughter, who is the sole heiress of all my property. Let us enter into an alliance. By this means not only will your debt be wiped out, but a sum to be fixed by yourself will be paid in addition, and I shall take care to improve your circumstances in general so far as lies in my power."

27

No one could be more joyous over this proposal than my father. Immediately, a contract was closed, in which the bride's dowry, as well as the required presents, was decided in accordance with my father's suggestion. The bill for the debt, which amounted to fifty thalers in Polish money, was returned to my father, and destroyed on the spot, while fifty thalers in addition were paid over to him.

Thereupon my new father-in-law went on to Nesvij to collect sundry debts there. Unfortunately he came to lodge at my former mother-in-law's. She, being a great prattler, volunteered information concerning the good match which her daughter had made. "The father of the bridegroom," said she, "is himself a great scholar, and the bridegroom is a young man of eleven years, who scarcely has his equal."

"I also," replied the landlord, "have, thank God, made a good choice for my daughter. You have perhaps heard of the celebrated scholar, Rabbi Joshua, in Mohilna, and of his young son, Solomon. Solomon is my daughter's bridegroom."

Hardly had these words been uttered, when she cried out, "That is a confounded lie. Solomon is my daughter's bridegroom; and here, sir, is the marriage contract."

The landlord then displayed his contract also; and they fell into a dispute, the result of which was that Madam Rissia had my father summoned before the court and demanded a categorical explanation. But my father failed to appear, although she had him summoned twice.

Meanwhile my mother died, and was brought to Nesvij for burial. My mother-in-law obtained a court order attaching the dead body, whereby interment was interdicted till the termination of the suit. My father found himself compelled to appear in court, my mother-in-law of course gained the suit, and I again became the groom of my former bride. And now to prevent any similar reversal of her plans in the future, and to take from my father all occasion for dissatisfaction, my mother-in-law endeavored to satisfy all his demands in accordance with her promise, clothed me from top to toe, and even paid my father for my board from the date of the betrothal to the marriage. My mother was now buried, and we returned home again.

My second father-in-law came too, and called upon my father for the fulfilment of his contract. Father pointed out that it was null and void, as it contravened a previous contract, and had been made by him in the supposition that my mother-in-law had no intention of fulfilling hers. The landlord seemed to give ear to these representations, to yield to necessity, and to reconcile himself to his loss; but in reality he was thinking of some means to get me into his hands. Accordingly, he rose by night, harnessed his horses, silently took me from the table on which I was sleeping, packed me with all despatch into his carriage, and made off with his booty out the gate. But as all this could not be accomplished without some noise, the people in the house awoke, discovered the theft, pursued the kidnapper, and snatched me out of his hand. At the time the whole incident appeared to me like a dream.

Thus my father was released from his debt, and received fifty thalers besides as a gratuity; but I was immediately afterwards carried off by my legal mother-in-law, and made the husband of my legal bride. I must confess that this transaction of my father's cannot be quite justified from a moral point of view. Only his great need at the time can in some measure serve to exculpate him.

CHAPTER X

The Secrets of Matrimony

ON THE FIRST EVENING OF MY MARRIAGE MY FATHER was not present. He had told me at my departure that he still had certain details to settle on my account, and that I must therefore await his arrival. Accordingly, I refused to appear that evening despite all pressure brought to bear upon me. The marriage festivities went on notwithstanding. We waited the next day for my father, but still he did not come. Then they threatened to bring a party of soldiers to drag me to the marriage ceremony; but I replied that if this were done it would avail them little, for the ceremony would not be lawful except as a voluntary act. At last, to the joy of all concerned, my father arrived towards evening, the details in question were amended, and the marriage ceremony was performed.

Here I must mention a little anecdote. I had read in a Hebrew book of an approved plan by which one spouse might secure lordship over the other for life. One was to tread on the other's foot at the marriage ceremony; and if both hit on the stratagem, the first to succeed would retain the upper hand. Accordingly, when my bride and I were placed side by side at the ceremony, this trick occurred to me, and I said to myself, "Now you must not let the opportunity pass of securing lordship over your wife for your whole lifetime." I was just going to tread on her foot, but a certain *je ne sais quoi*, whether fear, or shame, or love, held me back. While I was in this irresolute state, I suddenly felt my wife's slipper on my foot with such force that I should almost have screamed aloud if shame had not restrained me. I took this for a bad omen, and said to myself, "Providence has destined you to be the slave of your wife; you must not try to slip out of her fetters." From my faint-heartedness and the heroic mettle of my wife the reader may easily conceive why this prophecy had in fact to be realized.

But I was not only under the slipper of my wife, but—what was very much worse—under the lash of my mother-in-law. Nothing of all that she had promised was fulfilled. Her house, which she had settled on her daughter as a dowry, was burdened with debt. Of the six years' board which she had promised me I enjoyed scarcely half a year's, and this amid constant brawls and squabbles. Confident by reason of my youth and want of spirit, she even ventured now and again to lay hands on me, but this I repaid not infrequently with compound interest. Scarcely a meal passed during which we did not fling bowls, plates, spoons, and similar furniture at each other's head.

Once I came home from the academy ravenously hungry. As my mother-in-law and wife were occupied with the business of the tavern, I went myself where the milk was kept, and finding a dish of curds and cream, I fell upon it, and began to eat. My mother-in-law came as I was thus occupied, and shrieked in rage, "You are not going to devour the milk with the cream!" The more cream the better, thought I, and went on eating, without allowing myself to be disturbed by her screams. She was going to wrest the dish forcibly from my hands, beat me with her fists, and let me feel all her ill-will. Exasperated by such treatment, I thrust her from me, seized the dish, and smashed it on her head. That was a sight! The curds ran down all over her. In her rage she seized a scantling of wood, and if I had not speedily cleared out, she would certainly have beaten me to death.

Scenes like this were of frequent occurrence. At such skirmishes, of course, my wife had to remain neutral, and whichever party gained the upper hand it touched her very closely. "Oh!" she often complained, "if only the one or the other of you had a little more patience!"

Tired of a ceaseless open war I once hit upon a stratagem, which had good effect, at least for a short time. I rose about midnight, took a large earthenware vessel, crept with it under my mother-in-law's bed and began to speak aloud into the vessel after the following fashion: "O Rissia, Rissia, you ungodly woman, why do you treat my beloved son so ill? If you do not mend your ways, your end is near, and you will be damned to all eternity." Then I crept out again, and began to pinch her cruelly; and after a while I slipped silently back to bed.

The following morning she got up in consternation and told my wife that my mother had appeared to her in a dream and had threatened and pinched her on my account. In confirmation she showed the blue marks on her arm. When I came from the synagogue my mother-in-law was not at home, but I found my wife in tears. I asked the reason, but she would tell me nothing. My mother-in-law returned with a dejected look, her eyes red with weeping. She had gone, as I afterwards learned, to the Jewish burial ground, had thrown herself on my mother's grave, and had begged forgiveness of her fault. She then had the burial place measured, and ordered a wax taper as long as its circumference for burning in the synagogue.

he also fasted the whole day, and towards me she showed herself extremely amiable.

I knew what was the cause of the transformation, of course, but pretended not to observe it, and rejoiced in secret over the success of my stratagem. In this way I obtained peace for some time, but unfortunately not for long. The whole was soon forgotten again, and on the slightest occasion the dance would go on as before. In short, I was soon afterwards obliged to leave the house altogether, and accept a position as a private tutor. I would come home only for the great feast days.

In my fourteenth year my eldest son, David, was born to me. At my marriage I was only eleven years old, and owing to the retired life common among people of our nation in those regions, as well as the want of social contact between the sexes, I had no idea of the essential duties of marriage, but looked on a pretty girl as on any other work of nature or art. It was therefore natural that for a considerable time after marriage I could have no thought about its consummation. I used to approach my wife with trembling as an object of mystery. It was therefore supposed that I had been bewitched during the wedding; and under this supposition I was brought to a witch to be cured. She set on foot all sorts of operations, which of course had a good effect, although indirectly, by stimulating the imagination.

My life in Poland from my marriage to my emigration, which period embraces the springtime of my existence, was a series of manifold miseries. All means for the promotion of my development were wanting, and as a necessary corollary, my potentialities were aimlessly dissipated. The description of my then state causes my pen to drop from my hand, and I strive to stifle my painful memories.

The general constitution of Poland at the time; the condition of our people in it, who, like the poor ass with double burden, are oppressed by their own ignorance and the religious prejudices connected therewith, as well as by the ignorance and prejudices of the ruling classes; the misfortunes of my own family—all these causes combined to hinder the course of my progress, and to check the effect of my natural inclination.

CHAPTER XI

Striving for Culture amid Struggles with Misery

BY DINT OF INSTRUCTION RECEIVED FROM MY FATHER, but still more by my own industry, I had got on so well, that in my eleventh year I was able to pass as a full rabbi. I possessed besides some disconnected knowledge in history, astronomy, and other mathematical sciences. I burned with desire to acquire more knowledge, but how was this to be accomplished with the want of guidance, of scientific books, and of all other requisites? I was obliged to content myself with making use of any help that chance offered, without plan or method.

In order to gratify my desire of scientific knowledge the only means available was to learn foreign languages. But how was I to begin? To study Polish or Latin with a Catholic teacher was for me impossible, on the one hand, because the prejudices of my own people prohibited all languages but Hebrew and all sciences but the Talmud and the vast array of its commentators, and on the other hand, because the prejudices of Catholics would not allow them to give instruction in such subjects to a Jew. Moreover, my temporal circumstances were disheartening. I was obliged to support a whole family by teaching, by correcting proofs of the Holy Scriptures, and by other work of a similar nature. For a long time I could only sigh in vain for the satisfaction of my natural inclination.

At last a fortunate accident came to my help. I observed in some stout Hebrew volumes that they contained several alphabets, and that the number of their signatures was indicated not merely by Hebrew letters, but that for this purpose the characters of a second and a third alphabet had also been employed, these being commonly Latin and German. Now I had not the slightest idea of printing. I imagined that books were printed like linen, each page being the impression of a separate form. I presumed, however, that the characters which stood in corresponding places must represent one and the same letter, and as I had already heard something of the order of the alphabet in these languages, I supposed that, for example, *a*, standing in the same place as *aleph,* must likewise be an *aleph* in sound. In this way I gradually learnt the Latin and German characters.

By a kind of deciphering I began to combine various German letters into words; but as the characters corresponding to the Hebrew letters might be something quite different from the Hebrew, I was always in doubt whether the whole of my labor in this operation might not be in vain, till fortunately some leaves of an old German book fell into my hand. I began to read. How great were my joy and surprise when I saw from the connection, that the words completely corresponded with what I had learned. In my Jewish

language, to be sure, many of the words were unin
telligible; but from the context I was still able, eve
omitting such words, to comprehend the whole prett
well.

This mode of learning by deciphering still const
tutes my peculiar method of comprehending an
judging the thoughts of others. I maintain that no on
can say he understands a book as long as he finds hin
self compelled to deliver the author's thoughts in th
order and connection determined by the author, an
with the expressions which he has used. This is a mer
work of note, and no man can flatter himself with hav
ing comprehended an author till he is roused by hi
thoughts, which he apprehends at first but dimly, t
reflect on the subject himself, and to work it out fo
himself, though it may be under the impulse of an
other. This distinction between different kinds c
understanding must be evident to any man of discern
ment. For the same reason also I can understand
book only when the thoughts which it contains ha
monize after the intervening gaps are filled out.

CHAPTER XII

I Study the Kabbalah, and Even Become a Physician

KABBALAH, IN ITS WIDER SENSE, MEANS TRADITIO
and it comprehends not only the occult sciences whic
may not be taught publicly, but also the method
deducing new laws from those presented in Scriptur
as also some fundamental laws which are said to hav
been delivered orally to Moses on Mount Sinai. In t
narrower sense of the term, however, Kabbalah mea
only the tradition of occult sciences.

The principal work for the study of the Kabbalah

the *Zohar*, which is written in a very lofty style in the Syrian language. All other Kabbalistic writings are to be regarded as merely commentaries on the *Zohar* or extracts from it.

I learned that the junior rabbi or preacher of the place was an adept in the Kabbalah, and I therefore made his acquaintance. I took my seat beside him in the synagogue, and as I observed once that after prayer he always read from a small book, and then carefully put it back in its place, I became very curious to know what sort of book this was. Accordingly, after the preacher had gone home, I went and took the book from the place where he had put it; and when I found that it was a Kabbalistic work, I went with it and hid myself in a corner of the synagogue, till all the people had gone and the door was locked. I then crept from my hiding-place and, with no thought for food or drink the whole day long, read the fascinating book till the doorkeeper came in the evening and opened the synagogue again.

Shaare Kedushah, or *The Gates of Holiness,* was the title of this book; and, leaving out of account what was visionary and exaggerated, it contained the principal doctrines of psychology. I did with it therefore as the Talmudists say Rabbi Meir did with his heretic teacher: "He found a pomegranate, and he ate the fruit but cast the rind away."

By two or three days of such reading I finished the book; but instead of satisfying my curiosity, it only whetted it. I wished to read more books of the same sort. But as I was too bashful to confess this to the preacher, I resolved to write him a letter, in which I expressed my irresistible longing for this sacred science, and therefore entreated him earnestly to assist me with books. I received a very favorable reply. He praised my zeal for the sacred science, and assured me that this zeal, amid so little encouragement, was an obvious sign that my soul was derived from *Olam Atzilut* (the world of the immediate divine influence), while the souls of mere Talmudists take their origin from *Olam Yetzirah* (the world of the creation). He promised to assist me with books as far as lay in his power. But as he himself was mainly occupied with this science, and required to have such books constantly at hand, he could not lend them to me, but gave me permission to study them in his house at my pleasure.

Who was happier than I! I accepted the offer of the preacher with gratitude, scarcely ever left his house, and pored over the Kabbalistic books day and night. Two figures especially gave me great trouble. One was the *Tree*, or the representation of the divine emanations in their manifold and intricate complexities. The other was God's *Beard*, in which the hairs are divided into numerous classes with something peculiar to each, and every hair is a separate channel of divine grace. With all my efforts I could find no rational meaning in these representations.

My prolonged visits grew extremely inconvenient to the preacher. He had lately married a pretty young wife; and as his modest little home consisted of a single chamber, which was at once parlor, study, and bedroom, and as I sat in it at times reading the night through, it happened not infrequently that my elevation above the sphere of sense came into collision with his sensibility. Consequently he hit upon a good plan for getting rid of the incipient Kabbalist. He said to me one day, "I observe that it necessarily puts you to great inconvenience to spend your time constantly away from home for the sake of these books

You may take them home with you one by one if you please, and so study them at your convenience."

To me nothing could be more welcome. I took home one book after another, and studied them till I believed that I had mastered the whole of the Kabbalah. I contented myself not merely with the knowledge of its principles and manifold systems, but sought also to make a proper use of them. There was not a passage to be met with in the Holy Scriptures or in the Talmud the occult meaning of which I could not have unfolded, according to Kabbalistic principles, with the greatest readiness.

With the *Kabbalah Maasit,* or the *Practical Kabbalah,* I did not succeed so well as with the theoretical. The preacher boasted, not publicly indeed, but freely in private, that he was master of this also. Especially did he profess to be *roeh veeno nireh* (seeing but not seen), that is, to be able to make himself invisible.

For this trick I was especially eager, so that I might play practical jokes on my comrades with impunity. More particularly I formed a plan for keeping my ill-tempered mother-in-law in check by this means. I begged the preacher to impart the secret to me. I pretended that my object was merely to do good and guard against evil. The preacher consented, but at the same time said that certain preparations on my part were required. Three days in succession I was to fast, and each day to recite sundry *Yihudim*. These are Kabbalistic forms of prayer, whose occult meaning aims at producing in the intellectual world sexual unions by means of which certain results are to be brought about in the physical.

I performed the prescriptions cheerfully, made the conjuration which the preacher had taught me, and believed with all confidence that I was now invisible.

At once I hurried to the *Bet Hamidrash*, the Jewish academy, went up to one of my comrades, and gave him a vigorous box on the ear. He was not indolent, and returned the blow with interest. I started back in astonishment; I could not understand how he had been able to discover me, as I had observed the instructions of the preacher with the utmost accuracy. Still, I thought it possible I had unwittingly and unintentionally neglected some detail. I therefore resolved to undertake the operation anew. This time, however, I was not going to venture on the test of a box on the ear; I went into the academy merely to watch my comrades as a spectator. But as soon as I entered, one of them came up to me and showed me a difficult passage in the Talmud which he wished me to explain. I stood utterly confounded, and disconsolate over the disappointment of my hopes.

Thereupon I went to the preacher, and informed him of my want of success. Unblushing he replied quite boldly: "If you have observed all my instructions I cannot explain this otherwise than by supposing that you are unfit for being thus divested of the visibility of your body." Sorrowfully I was obliged to give up entirely the hope of making myself invisible.

This disappointed hope was followed by a new delusion. In the preface to the *Book of Raziel*, which the angel of that name is said to have delivered to our first father Adam at his banishment from paradise, I found the promise that whoever keeps the book in his house is thereby insured against fire. It was not long, however, before a conflagration broke out in the neighborhood, and the fire seized my house too, so that the angel Raziel himself had to ascend to heaven in the chariot of fire.

Unsatisfied with the literary knowledge of the

science, I sought to penetrate into its spirit; and as I perceived that the whole science, if it deserves to be called such, can contain nothing but the secrets of nature concealed in fables and allegories, I labored to discover these secrets, and so raise my merely literary knowledge to a rational knowledge. Fortunately I learned that the chief rabbi of a neighboring town who had lived in Germany for a while as a young man and had there learned the German language, and had obtained some acquaintance with the sciences, continued still, though in secret, to work at the sciences, and possessed a fair library of German books.

I resolved therefore to make a pilgrimage to S....., in order to see the chief rabbi and beg a few scientific books of him. I was tolerably accustomed to such journeys, and had once gone thirty miles on foot to see a Hebrew work of the tenth century on the Peripatetic philosophy. Without troubling myself in the least about traveling expenses or means of conveyance, therefore, and without saying a word to my family, I set out upon the journey to this town in the heart of winter. As soon as I arrived, I went to the chief rabbi, told him my desire, and begged him earnestly for assistance. He was not a little astonished, for during the thirty-one years which had elapsed since his return from Germany not a soul had ever made such a request. He promised to lend me some old German books. The most important among these were an old work on optics, and Sturm's *Physics*.

I could not sufficiently express my gratitude to the excellent rabbi; I pocketed the few books, and returned home in rapture. After I had studied these books thoroughly, my eyes were suddenly opened. I believed that I had found a key to all the secrets of nature, as I now knew the nature of storms, of dew, of rain, and other such phenomena. In my pride I looked down on all others who did not yet know these things, laughed at their prejudices and superstitions, and proposed to clear up their ideas on these subjects and to enlighten their understanding.

On one occasion I went for a walk with some friends. It chanced that a goat lay in our road. I struck the goat some blows with my stick, and my friends chided me for my cruelty. "Where is the cruelty?" I replied. "Do you believe that the goat feels pain when I beat it? You are greatly mistaken; the goat is a mere machine." This was the doctrine of Sturm, who was a disciple of Descartes. My friends laughed heartily, and said, "But don't you hear the goat cry when you beat it?" "Yes," I replied, "of course it cries; but if you beat a drum, it cries too." They were amazed at my answer, and in a short time it was spread abroad over the whole town that I had gone mad, as I held that a goat is a drum.

From my generous friend, the chief rabbi, I subsequently received two medical works, Kulm's *Anatomical Tables* and Voit's *Gaziopilatium*. The latter is a large medical dictionary, containing, in a brief form, not only explanations in all departments of medicine, but also their manifold applications. In connection with every disease explanations of its cause, symptoms, and the method of its cure are given, along with the ordinary prescriptions. This was a real treasure. I studied the book thoroughly, and believed myself to be master of the science of medicine and a complete physician.

But I was not going to content myself with mere theory in this matter; I resolved to make regular application of it. I visited patients, determined all diseases according to their circumstances and symptoms, explained their causes, and also gave prescriptions for their cure. But in this practice things turned out very comically. If a patient told me some of the symptoms of his disease, I deduced the nature of the disease itself, and inferred the presence of other symptoms. If the patient said that he could feel none of these, I stubbornly insisted on their being present all the same. Our conversation sometimes came to this:

I. "You have a headache also."

Patient. "No."

I. "But you *must* have a headache."

As many symptoms are common to several diseases, I frequently took *quid pro quo.* Prescriptions I could never keep in my head, so that when I was to prescribe anything, I was obliged to go home first and turn up my *Gaziopilatium.* At length I even began to make up drugs myself according to Voit's prescriptions. How this succeeded may be imagined. It had at least this good result, that I saw something more was surely required for a practical physician than I understood at the time.

CHAPTER XIII

Jewish Piety and Penances

IN MY YOUTH I POSSESSED A RELIGIOUS DISPOSITION; AND as I observed much pride, quarrelsomeness, and other evil traits in most of the rabbis, I grew to dislike them on that account. Hence I sought models only among those who are commonly known by the name of *Hasidim,* or *the Pious.* These devote the whole of their lives to the strictest observances of the laws and moral virtues. Afterwards I had occasion to remark that for their part these men do less harm indeed to *others,* but all the greater to *themselves,* inasmuch as they throw the baby out with the bath-water. In seeking to suppress their desires and passions, they also suppress their powers and cramp their activity, to the degree that their exercises frequently bring them to an untimely death.

Two or three instances, of which I was myself an eyewitness, will be sufficient for demonstration. A Jewish scholar at that time well known on account of his piety, Simon of Lubtsch, had undergone the severest exercises of penance. He had already carried out the *Teshuvat Hakana* (the penance of Kana), which consists in fasting daily for six years, and avoiding the use of anything that derives from a living being (flesh, milk, honey, and the like) for the evening meal. He had also practiced *Galut,* that is, a continuous wandering, in which the penitent is not allowed to remain two days in the same place. In addition, he had worn a hairshirt next to his body. But he felt that he would not satisfy his conscience unless he further observed the *Teshuvat Hamishkal* (the penance of weighing), which requires a particular form of penance proportioned to every sin. But as he found by calculation that the number of his sins was too great to be atoned for in this way, he took it into his head to starve himself to death. After he had spent some time in this process, he came in his wanderings to the place where my father lived, and, unbeknownst to the household, went into the barn, where he fell to the ground in a dead faint. My father chanced to come into the barn, and found the man, whom he had long known, lying on the ground half dead with a *Zohar* (the principal book of the Kabbalists) in his hand. As he knew well what sort of man this was, he brought him all sorts of refreshments at once; but the man would make no use of them whatever. My father came again and again and begged Simon to take something, but all in vain. My father had to attend to something in the house, where-upon Simon, to escape from his importunity, exerted all his strength, raised himself up, went out of the barn, and at last out of the village. When my father returned to the barn and found the man no longer there, he ran after him, and found him lying dead not far from the village. The affair was generally made known among the Jews, and Simon became a saint.

Yossel of Klezk proposed nothing less than to hasten the advent of the Messiah. To this end he performed strict penance, fasted, rolled himself in snow, under-took nightwatches and similar austerities. By pursuits of this sort he believed he could accomplish the over-throw of the legion of evil spirits who kept guard on the Messiah and obstructed his coming.

CHAPTER XIV

Friendship and *Schwärmerei*

IN THE PLACE WHERE I RESIDED I HAD A BOSOM FRIEND, Moses Lapidoth by name. We were of the same age, had pursued the same studies, and under nearly the same external circumstances. The only difference be-tween us was that I soon showed an inclination to the sciences, while Lapidoth had indeed a love of specula-tion along with great acuteness and discernment, but he had no wish to proceed further than he could reach by a mere sound common sense. With this friend I used to hold many a conversation on subjects of mu-tual interest, especially questions of religion and morals.

We were the only persons in the place who ventured to think independently about everything and not be mere imitators. Differing as we did from the rest of the community in our opinions and conduct, it was natural that we should separate ourselves from them by degrees. But we still had to live by the community, and so our circumstances deteriorated daily. We saw where our inclinations were leading us, to be sure, but were nevertheless unwilling to sacrifice them to material advantage. We consoled ourselves for our loss as best we might, spoke constantly of the vanity of all things, and of the religious and moral shortcomings of the common herd, upon whom we looked down with a sort of noble pride and condescension.

We used especially to expatiate, *à la* Mandeville, on the hollowness of human virtue. For example, there had been a smallpox epidemic, which had carried off many children. The elders assembled to find out the secret sins for which, in their view, the visitation was a retribution. Upon inquiry it was found that a young Jewish widow was in too easy relations with certain servants of the manor. She was summoned, but no sort of inquisition could elicit from her anything beyond the story that these people were in the habit of drinking ale in her house, and she naturally received them pleasantly and politely; beyond this she was conscious of no sin. As no evidence was forthcoming, she was about to be acquitted, when an elderly matron came flying in like a fury and screamed, "Scourge her! Scourge her till she has confessed her sin! If you do not, then may guilt for the death of so many innocent souls fall upon you!" Lapidoth was present with me at this scene, and said, "Friend, do you suppose that Madam is making so fierce an onslaught against this woman merely because she is seized with holy zeal and concern for the general welfare? Oh no! She is enraged merely because the widow still possesses attractions, while she herself can no longer pretend to any." I assured him that I agreed with his judgment completely.

Lapidoth's parents-in-law were poor. His father-in-law was a Jewish sexton, and his slender pay was sorry support for his family. Every Friday the poor man was compelled to listen to his wife's violent reproach and abuse because he could not provide her with the necessaries for the holy Sabbath. Lapidoth told me his story, and added, "My mother-in-law wants me to believe that her zeal is wholly for the honor of the holy Sabbath. Nay, verily; her zeal is wholly for the honor of her own holy paunch, which she cannot fill as she would like; the holy Sabbath merely serves her as a pretext."

Once, upon a walk on the wall which encircled the town, we were conversing about the tendency, illustrated by this and other instances, for men to deceive themselves and others on the score of their true motives. I said to Lapidoth, "Friend, let us be fair and pass our censure on ourselves as well as on others. Is not the contemplative life which we lead, so ill-adapted to our circumstances, to be regarded as a result of our indolence and inclination to idleness, which we seek to defend by reflections on the vanity of all things? We are content with our present circumstances; why? Because we cannot alter them without first overcoming our inclination to idleness. With all our pretense of contempt for things external, we cannot avoid the secret wish to be able to enjoy better food and clothing than at present. We reproach our friends as vain men addicted to the pleasures of the senses, because they eschew our mode of life and undertake occupations consonant with their powers. But where is our superiority, when we merely follow our inclination as they follow theirs? Let us seek to find this superiority solely in the fact that we at least confess this truth to ourselves, while they profess as the motive of their actions not the satisfaction of their own particular desires but the impulse to the general welfare." Lapidoth, who was deeply impressed by my remarks, answered with some warmth, "Friend, you are perfectly right. If we cannot now mend our faults, we will at any rate not deceive ourselves about them, but at least keep the way open for amendment."

But this enthusiastic companionship, like everything else in the world, had to come to an end. As we were both married and our marriages fruitful, we were obliged, in order to support our families, to accept situations as family tutors. This led to frequent separations, and soon we were able to be together only a few weeks in the year.

CHAPTER XV

The Life of a Family Tutor

MY FIRST POSITION AS FAMILY TUTOR WAS AN HOUR'S distance from my home. The family was that of a miserable farmer in a still more miserable village; and my salary was five thalers in Polish money. The poverty, ignorance, and crudeness which prevailed in this house were indescribable. The farmer himself was a man of about fifty years, the whole of whose face was overgrown with hair, ending in a dirty, thick beard, as black as pitch. His language was a sort of muttering, intelligible only to the boors with whom he daily associated. Not only was he ignorant of Hebrew, but he could not speak a word of Yiddish; his only language was Russian, the common patois of the peasantry. His wife and children were of the same stamp. Their home was a hovel of smoke, black as coal within and without, with no chimney, but merely a small aperture in the roof for the smoke; this opening was carefully closed as soon as the fire died down, so that the heat might not escape.

In this magnificent dwelling the peasants sit on the bare ground; you dare not sit higher if you do not wish to be suffocated with the smoke. Here they guzzle their whiskey and make an uproar, while the people of the house sit in a corner. I usually took my place behind the stove with my dirty, half-naked pupils, and expounded to them out of an old tattered Bible, from Hebrew into Russian-Yiddish. All this made such a splendid group as deserved to be sketched only by a Hogarth, and to be sung only by a Butler.

It may be easily imagined how wretched my condition here must have been. Brandy became my sole comfort, and made me forget all my misery. To top all, a regiment of Russians, who were then rioting with every conceivable cruelty on the estates of Prince Radzivil, was stationed in the village and its vicinity. The house was constantly full of drunken Russians, who committed all sorts of excesses, hewed tables and benches to pieces, hurled glasses and bottles into the faces of their hosts, and so on. My other positions as tutor were more or less similar.

CHAPTER XVI

A Secret Society: the Hasidic Sect

ABOUT THIS TIME I BECAME ACQUAINTED WITH A SECT of my people called the *New Hasidim*, which was then coming into prominence. Hasidim is the name generally given by the Hebrews to the *pious*, that is, to those who are distinguished by the exercise of the

49

strictest piety. From time immemorial men such as these have freed themselves from worldly occupations and pleasures and devoted their lives to the strictest observance of the laws of religion and to penance for their sins. They sought to attain this object, as has been said above, by prayers and other exercises of devotion, by chastisement of the body, and by similar means.

But about this time some among them set themselves up as founders of a new sect. They maintained that true piety by no means consists in chastisement of the body, by which the spiritual quiet and cheerfulness necessary to the knowledge and love of God are disturbed. On the contrary, they maintained that man must satisfy all his bodily wants and take such enjoyment of pleasures of sense as may be necessary for the development of our perceptions, inasmuch as God has created all for his glory. True service of God, in their view, consists in exercises of devotion with exertion of all our powers, and annihilation of self before God; for they maintain that man, in accordance with his destiny, can reach highest perfection only when he regards himself not as a being existing and working in and for itself, but as an organ of the Godhead. Instead of spending their lives in separation from the world, suppressing their natural feelings, and deadening their powers, they believed that they acted much more to the purpose in seeking to develop their natural feelings as fully as possible, to bring their powers into exercise, and constantly to widen their sphere of activity.

Those of the first sect press their penitential urge to an extravagant degree. Instead of merely regulating their desires and passions by rules of moderation, they seek to annihilate them; and instead of endeavoring, like the Stoics, to find the principle of their actions in pure reason, they seek it rather in religion. This is a pure source, it is true; but as these people have false ideas of religion itself, and their virtue has as its basis merely the future rewards and punishments of an arbitrary tyrannical being who governs by mere caprice, their actions in point of fact flow from an impure source, namely the principle of interest. Moreover, in their case this interest rests merely on fancies; so that, in this respect, they are far below the grossest Epicureans, who have a low, to be sure, but nevertheless genuine interest as the end of their actions. Only when it is itself founded on the idea of virtue can religion yield a principle of virtue.

The ideas of the second sect on religion and morals are indeed better founded; but since their conduct is guided for the most part by obscure feelings rather than distinct knowledge, they likewise necessarily fall into all manner of extravagance. Self-annihilation inevitably cramps their activity, or gives it false direction. They have no natural science, no acquaintance with psychology; and they are vain enough to consider themselves organs of the Godhead—which, of course, they are, but to an extent limited by the degree of perfection they attain. The result is, that at the charges of the Godhead they perpetrate the greatest excesses; every extraordinary suggestion is to them a divine inspiration, and every lively impulse a divine call.

Those sects were not in fact distinct sects of religion; their difference consisted merely in the mode of their religious exercises. But still their animosity went so far that they condemned each other as heretics, and indulged in mutual persecution. At first the new sect held the upper hand, and spread over nearly the whole of Poland, and even beyond. The heads of the sect sent regular emissaries everywhere, whose duty it

51

was to preach the new doctrine and win converts. Now the majority of the Polish Jews consist of scholars, that is, men devoted to an inactive and contemplative life; for every Polish Jew is destined from his birth to be a rabbi, and only the greatest incapacity can exclude him from that rank. Moreover, this new doctrine was calculated to make the way to blessedness easier, inasmuch as it declared that fasts and vigils and the constant study of the Talmud are not only useless, but even prejudicial to that cheerfulness of spirit which is essential to genuine piety. It was therefore natural that the adherents of the doctrine quickly multiplied. The rapid spread of this sect and the favor with which a great part of the people regarded it may be very easily explained. The natural inclination to idleness and a life of speculation on the part of the majority, who from birth are destined to study; the dryness and unfruitfulness of rabbinical studies; the great burden of the ceremonial law, which the new doctrine promised to lighten and finally, the tendency to fanaticism and the love of the marvelous, which are nurtured by this doctrine—these are sufficient to make this phenomenon intelligible.

I could form no accurate idea of the new sect, and did not know what to think of it, till I met with a young man who had already been initiated into the society and had enjoyed the good fortune of conversing with high personages face to face. This man happened to be traveling through the town I lived in, and I seized the opportunity of asking for information on the internal constitution of the society, the mode of admission, and so forth. The stranger was still in the lowest grade of membership, and consequently knew nothing about the internal constitution of the society and could give me no information on the subject. But for the mode of admission, he assured me that that was the simplest thing in the world. Anyone who felt a desire of perfection, but did not know how to satisfy it, or wished to remove hindrances to its satisfaction, had only to apply to the superiors of the society, and *eo ipso* he became a member. He need not even tell of his past, as one must do on applying to a medical doctor; he need say nothing to these superiors about his moral weakness, his previous character, and matters of that sort, inasmuch as nothing was unknown to the superiors. They could see into the human heart, and discern all that is concealed in its secret recesses; they could foretell the future, and bring near things remote.

I could not restrain my astonishment at the exquisite refinement of these thoughts, and consequently I wished nothing so much as the pleasure of becoming a member of this honorable society. Therefore I resolved to undertake a journey to M......, where the superior B...... resided. Impatiently I waited for the close of my term of service, which still had some weeks to run. As soon as this was finished, instead of going home (though I was only two miles away), I started at once on my pilgrimage. The journey extended over some weeks.

At last I arrived at M......, and after having rested from my journey I went to the house of the superior with the notion that I could be introduced to him at once. I was told, however, that he could not speak to me at the time, but that I was invited to his table on Sabbath along with the other strangers who had come to visit him: I should then have the happiness of seeing the saintly man face to face and of hearing the sublimest teachings out of his own mouth; although this was a public audience, yet, on account of the individual references which I should find made to myself, I might regard it as a special interview.

Accordingly, on Sabbath I went to this solemn meal, and there found a large number of respectable men who had gathered together from various quarters. At length the great man appeared, his awe-inspiring figure clothed in white satin. Even his shoes and snuffbox were white, this being among the Kabbalists the color of grace. He greeted each newcomer with Shalom. We sat down to table and during the meal a solemn silence reigned. After the meal was over, the superior struck up a solemn inspiriting melody, held his hand for some time upon his brow, and then began to call out, "Z. . . . . . of H. . . . . ., M. . . . . . of R. . . . . ., S. M. of N. . . . . .," and so on. Each newcomer was thus called by his own name and the name of his residence, which excited no little astonishment. Each as he was called recited some verse of the Holy Scriptures. Thereupon the superior began to deliver a sermon for which the verses recited served as a text, so that although they were disconnected verses taken from different parts of Scripture they were combined with as much skill as if they had formed a single whole. What was still more extraordinary, every one of the newcomers believed that he discovered in that part of the sermon which was founded on his verse something that had special reference to the facts of his own spiritual life. At this we were of course greatly astonished.

It was not long, however, before I began to qualify the high opinion I had formed of this superior and the whole society. I observed that their ingenious exegesis was at bottom false, and, furthermore, limited strictly to their own extravagant principles, such as the doctrine of self-annihilation. Having once learned this doctrine, there was nothing new for a man to hear. The alleged miracles could be very naturally explained. By means of correspondence and spies and a certain knowledge of men, by observing a man's physiognomy and by skillful questioning, the superiors were able to elicit indirectly the secrets of the heart, so that among these simple men they succeeded in obtaining the reputation of inspired prophets.

The whole society also displeased me not a little by their cynical spirit and the excess of their merriment. A single example may suffice. We had once met at the hour of prayer in the house of the superior. One of the company arrived somewhat late, and the others asked his reason. He replied that he had been detained by his wife having been that evening delivered of a daughter. As soon as they heard this, they began to congratulate him in an uproarious fashion. The superior thereupon came out of his study and asked the cause of the noise. He was told that we were congratulating our friend because his wife had brought a girl into the world. "A girl!" he answered with the greatest indignation. "He ought to be whipped." (A trait of these, as of all uncultivated men, is their contempt for the other sex.) The poor fellow protested. He could not comprehend why he should be made to suffer for his wife having brought a girl into the world. But this was of no avail: he was seized, thrown down on the floor, and whipped unmercifully. All except the victim fell into an hilarious mood over the affair, upon which the superior called them to prayer in the following words, "Now, brethren, serve the Lord with gladness!"

I would not stay in the place any longer. I sought the superior's blessing, took my departure from the society, resolved to abandon it forever, and returned home.

CHAPTER XVII

Journeys to Koenigsberg, Stettin and Berlin, to Learn the Ways of Men

MY EXTERNAL CIRCUMSTANCES WERE STEADILY BECOMING worse. I was unwilling to adapt myself to my ordinary occupations any longer, and hence found myself everywhere out of my sphere. On the other hand, my town afforded little means to satisfy my yearning for study of the sciences. And I determined to betake myself to Germany, there to study medicine and, as opportunity offered, other sciences as well. But the question was, how so long a journey was to be made. I knew indeed that certain merchants of my town were soon to make a journey to Koenigsberg in Prussia; my acquaintance with them was slight and I could not expect that they would take me with them gratis. After much deliberation I hit upon a capital expedient at last.

Among my friends there was a very learned and devout man, who enjoyed great esteem among all the Jews of the town. I revealed my purpose to him, and solicited his counsel. He went to a merchant of his acquaintance, represented to him the importance of my undertaking, and persuaded him to take me with him to Koenigsberg on his own vessel. The merchant could refuse nothing to so godly a man, and so gave his consent.

Accordingly, I set out with this Jewish merchant for Koenigsberg in Prussia. When I arrived there, I went to the Jewish medical doctor of the place, broached my proposal to study medicine, and begged his advice and support. As his professional preoccupations prevented him from conveniently speaking with me on the subject, and as he could not in any case understand me well, he referred me to certain students who lodged in his house. As soon as I showed myself to these young gentlemen, and revealed my intentions, they burst into loud laughter. And certainly they were not to be blamed. Imagine a man from Polish Lithuania of about five-and-twenty years, with a tolerably stiff beard, in tattered dirty clothes, whose language is a mixture of Hebrew, Yiddish, Polish, and Russian, with their several grammatical inaccuracies, who gives it out that he understands the German language, and that he has attained some knowledge of the sciences. What were the young gentlemen to think?

They began to poke fun at me, and gave me Mendelssohn's *Phaedon* to read, which by chance lay on the table. My reading was pitiful, both on account of the peculiar manner in which I had learned the German language, and on account of my bad pronunciation. Again they burst into loud laughter; but said I must explain what I had read. This I did in my own fashion; but as they did not understand me, they demanded that I should translate what I had read into Hebrew. This I did on the spot. The students, who understood Hebrew well, fell into no slight astonishment when they saw that I had not only grasped correctly the meaning of this celebrated author, but also expressed it happily in Hebrew. They then began to take interest in my welfare, and procured me cast-off clothing and board during my stay in Koenigsberg. At the same time they advised me to go to Berlin, where I should best attain my object. To make the journey suit my circumstances, however, they advised me to go by ship from Koenigsberg to Stettin, and thence to Frankfort on the Oder, from which place I should easily find means of getting to Berlin.

And so I went by ship, having no food except dry biscuit, some herring, and a flask of spirits. In Koenigsberg I had been told that the journey might take ten or at the most fourteen days. But this prognosis was wrong. By reason of contrary winds the voyage lasted five weeks. My state may be easily imagined. There were no other passengers on the vessel but an old woman, who sang hymns all the time for solace. The Pomeranian German of the crew I could understand as little as they could my medley of Yiddish, Polish, and Lithuanian. I got nothing warm to eat the whole time, and was obliged to sleep on hard stuffed bags. On occasion the vessel was near foundering. Of course I was seasick most of the time.

At last I arrived at Stettin, whence I had been told I could easily make the journey to Frankfort on foot. But how was a Polish Jew in the most wretched circumstances, without a penny for food and without knowing the language of the country, to make a journey even of a few miles? Yet it had to be done. Accordingly, I set out from Stettin, and as I thought over my miserable situation, I sat down under a lime tree, and began to weep bitterly. My spirit soon became somewhat lighter; I took courage, and went on. After I had gone some miles, I arrived towards evening at an inn, quite exhausted. It was the eve of the Jewish fast which falls in August. Already I was nearly starving with hunger and thirst, and I was still to fast the whole of the next day. I had not a penny to spend and nothing of any value to sell.

After long reflection it occurred to me that I must still have in my coat pocket an iron spoon, which I had taken with me on board ship. I brought it, and begged the landlady of the inn to give me a little bread and beer for it. At first she refused to take the spoon, but after much importunity she was at last induced to grant a glass of sour beer in exchange. I was obliged to content myself with this, drank my glass of beer, and went off to the stable to sleep on straw.

In the morning I proceeded on my journey, having previously inquired for a place where Jews were to be found, so that I might be able to go to synagogue, and join with my brethren in chanting the lamentations over the destruction of Jerusalem. This was done, and after the prayers and singing, about midday, I went to the Jewish schoolmaster of the place, and had some conversation with him. He soon discovered that I was a full rabbi, began to interest himself in my case, and procured me a supper at the house of a Jew. He also gave me a letter of introduction to another schoolmaster in the neighboring town, recommending me as a great Talmudist and an honorable rabbi. Here also I met with a fair reception. I was invited to the Sabbath dinner by the most respectable and richest Jew of the place, and went into the synagogue, where I was shown to the choicest pew, and received every mark of honor usually bestowed on a rabbi.

After the close of the service the rich Jew referred to took me to his house, and put me in the place of honor at his table, that is, between himself and his daughter. She was a young girl of about twelve years, dressed in the most beautiful style. I began, as rabbi, to hold a very learned and edifying discourse; and the less the gentleman and lady understood it, the more divine it seemed to them. All at once I observed, to my chagrin, that the young lady began to put on a sour look, and to make wry faces. At first I did not know how to explain this; but, after a while, when I turned my eyes upon myself and my miserable dirty suit of rags, the whole mystery was at once unriddled. The uneasiness of the young lady had a very good cause. And how could it be otherwise? Since I left

Koenigsberg, about seven weeks before, I had never had a clean shirt to put on; and I had been obliged to lie in the stables of inns on bare straw, on which who knows how many poor travelers had lain before. Now all at once I realized my misery in its appalling magnitude. But what was I to do? How was I to help myself out of this unfortunate situation? Gloomy and sad, I soon bade farewell to these good people, and proceeded on my journey to Berlin, struggling continually with want and misery of every kind.

At last I reached Berlin. Here I believed that I should put an end to my misery, and accomplish all my wishes. Alas, I was sadly deceived. In this capital, as everyone knows, no Jewish beggars were allowed. Accordingly, the Jewish community of the place, in order to make provision for their poor, have built a house at the Rosenthaler Gate, where the poor are received and questioned by the Jewish elders concerning their intentions in Berlin. According to the results of such inquiry, visitors are either taken into the city, if they are sick or want employment, or they are sent forward on their journey. I was duly brought to this house, which was filled partly with sick people, partly with a wretched rabble. For a long while I looked round in vain for someone with whom I might talk about my affairs.

At last I observed a man who, to judge by his dress, was surely a rabbi. I approached him, and was overjoyed to learn from him that he was indeed a rabbi, and very well known in Berlin! I conversed with him on all sorts of subjects connected with rabbinical learning; and as I was very openhearted, I related to him the course of my life in Poland, revealed to him my purpose of studying medicine in Berlin, showed him my commentary on the *Moreh Nebukhim*, and so forth. He listened attentively, and seemed to interest himself very much in my behalf. But all at once he disappeared from sight.

At length towards evening came the Jewish elders. Each of the persons in the house was called, and questioned about his wants. When my turn came, I said quite frankly that I wished to remain in Berlin in order to study medicine. The elders refused my request point-blank, gave me a pittance in charity, and went away.

The explanation for their attitude towards me in particular was as follows: The rabbi of whom I spoke was a zealot in his orthodoxy. Accordingly, when he had discovered my sentiments and purposes, he went into town and informed the elders about my heretical mode of thinking. He told them that I was going to issue a new edition of the *Moreh Nebukhim* with a commentary, and that my intention was not so much to study medicine, but mainly to devote myself to the sciences in general, and to extend my knowledge. This the orthodox Jews look upon as a thing dangerous to religion and good morals. They are especially concerned for the Polish rabbis who, having by some lucky accident been delivered from the bondage of superstition, suddenly catch a gleam of the light of reason and set themselves free from their chains. And this concern is to some degree well-founded. Persons in such a position are like a man who has long been famished and suddenly comes upon a well-spread table; such a man will attack the food with violent greed, and fill himself to surfeit.

The refusal of permission to stay in Berlin came upon me like a thunderclap. The ultimate object of all my hopes and wishes was all at once removed beyond my reach, just when I had seen it so near. I found myself in the situation of Tantalus, and did not know where to turn for help. I was especially pained by the treatment I received from the overseer of the poorhouse, who, by command of his superiors, urged my speedy departure, and never left off till he saw me outside of the gate. There I threw myself on the ground and began to weep bitterly. It was a Sunday, and many people were going walking outside of the city. Most of them never turned aside to a whining worm like me, but some compassionate souls were very much struck with the sight, and asked the cause of my wailing. I answered them; but, partly on account of my unintelligible language, partly because my speech was broken by frequent weeping and sobbing, they could not understand what I said.

I was so deeply affected by this vexation that I fell into a violent fever. The soldiers who kept guard at the gate reported this at the poorhouse. The overseer came and carried me in. I stayed there over the day, and made myself glad with the hope of becoming thoroughly sick, so as to enforce a longer sojourn in the place, during which I thought I might form some acquaintances by whose influence I hoped to receive protection and permission to remain in Berlin. But alas! in this hope I was deceived. The following day I rose quite lively again without a trace of fever. I was therefore obliged to go. But whither? That I did not know myself. Accordingly, I took the first road that I came upon, and surrendered myself to fate.

CHAPTER XVIII

Deepest Misery and Deliverance

IN THE EVENING I CAME TO AN INN, WHERE I MET A POOR tramp who was a Jewish beggar by profession. I was uncommonly pleased to meet one of my brethren with whom I could talk and to whom this neighborhood was pretty well known. I therefore resolved to wander about the countryside with this companion and so keep body and soul together, though two such heterogeneous persons were nowhere to be met in the world. I was an educated rabbi; he was an idiot. I had hitherto maintained myself in an honorable way; he was a beggar by profession. I had ideas of morality, propriety, and decency; he knew nothing of these. Finally, I was in sound health, to be sure, but still of weakly constitution; he, on the other hand, was a sturdy, able-bodied fellow, who would have made the best of soldiers.

Notwithstanding these differences, I stuck close to the man, since to stay alive I was compelled to become a vagrant in a strange land. In our wandering I labored to communicate to my companion ideas of religion and of true morality, while he in return instructed me in the art of begging. He taught me the usual formulas of the art, and recommended me especially to curse and swear, whenever I was sent away empty-handed.

In this way we wandered about in a district of a few miles for nearly half a year. At last we resolved to turn our steps towards Poland. When we arrived at Posen, we took up our quarters in the Jewish poorhouse, the master of which was a poor mending tailor. Here I formed the resolve to bring my wandering to a close, whatever the cost. It was harvest time, and already began to be pretty cold. I was almost naked and barefoot. The vagrant life had impaired my health, for I never got regular meals, for the most part had to content myself with bits of mouldy bread and water, and at night was obliged to lie on old straw, sometimes even on the bare earth. Besides, the sacred seasons and fast days in the Jewish calendar were coming on; and as at that time I was quite religious, I could not endure the thought of passing in complete idleness the period which others employed for the welfare of their souls.

And so I resolved, at least for the present, to go no further, and, if worst should come to worst, to throw myself before the synagogue, and either die there or excite the compassion of my brethren and so bring my sufferings to an end. Consequently, as soon as my comrade awoke in the morning, began to prepare for a begging tour, and bade me join him, I told him that I would not go with him. When he asked how else I proposed to sustain life, I was able to answer nothing but "God will surely help."

I then went off to the Jewish school. Here I found a number of pupils, some of whom were reading while others took advantage of the master's absence to pass the time in play. I also took a book to read. The pupils were struck by my strange dress, and approached to ask whence I came and what I wanted. Their questions I answered in my Lithuanian dialect, at which they began to laugh and make merry at my expense. For this I cared little. But I recollected that, some years before, a chief rabbi from my neighborhood had been appointed to the same office in Posen, and that he had taken with him a good friend of mine as his secretary. Accordingly, I asked the boys about this friend. To my extreme sorrow I learned that he was no longer in Posen, as the chief rabbi[1] had afterwards been called to the same office in Hamburg, and his secretary had gone with him to that place. They told me, however, that his son, a boy about twelve years old, had been left behind in Posen with the present chief rabbi,[2] who was a son-in-law of his predecessor.

This information saddened me not a little. Still, the last circumstance gave me some hope. I inquired after the dwelling of the new chief rabbi, and went there; but as I was almost naked I shrank from entering, and waited until I saw someone going into the house, whom I begged to be so good as to call my friend's son out. The boy recognized me at once, and manifested his astonishment at seeing me there in such a pitiable plight. I replied that this was not the time to relate all the misfortunes which had brought me to this state, and that at present he should consider merely how he might relieve my distress somewhat.

This he promised to do. He went to the chief rabbi, and announced me as a great scholar and a pious man, who by extraordinary accidents had fallen into a very miserable condition. The chief rabbi, who was an excellent man, an acute Talmudist, and of very gentle character, was touched by my distress, and sent for me to come in. He conversed with me awhile, discussing some of the most important questions of the Talmud, and found me well versed in all branches of Jewish learning. Then he inquired about my intentions, and I told him that I wished to be introduced as a tutor into some family, but that meanwhile my only desire was to be able to celebrate the sacred season here, and for this short period at least to interrupt my travels.

The good-hearted rabbi bade me, so far as this was

1 Rafael Kohen, chief rabbi in Posen, 1774-1776.
2 Zevi Hirsch ben Abraham.

concerned, to lay all anxiety aside, spoke of my desire as a small matter, which it was nothing more than reasonable to want. He then gave me what money he had by him, invited me to dine with him every Sabbath as long as I remained in Posen, and bade his boy procure a respectable lodging for me. The boy soon returned and conducted me to my lodging. I expected this to be only a small chamber in the house of some poor man. I was therefore not a little astonished when I found myself in the house of one of the most distinguished Jews of the town, and that there had been prepared for me a neat little room, which was the study of the master, he and his son both being scholars.

As soon as I had looked round a little, I went to the housewife, and thrusting some coppers into her hand, I asked her to get me some gruel for supper. She began to smile at my simplicity, and said, "No, no, sir! that is not our agreement. The chief rabbi has not given you such a recommendation that you are obliged to have us making you gruel for money." She then went on to explain that I was not only to lodge in her house, but also to eat and drink with them as long as I stayed in the town. I was astonished at this unexpected good fortune; but my delight was still greater when after supper I was shown to a clean bed. I could not believe my eyes, and asked several times, "Is this really for me?" I can say with truth that never before or since have I felt such a degree of happiness as when I lay down that night and felt my limbs, which for half a year had been overwearied and almost broken, recovering their former strength in a soft bed.

I slept till late in the day. I had scarcely risen when the chief rabbi sent for me to come and see him. When I made my appearance, he asked me how I was pleased with my lodging. I could not find words to express my feelings, and exclaimed in ecstasy, "I have slept in a bed!" At this the chief rabbi was uncommonly pleased. He then sent for the cantor, and as soon as this man appeared, he said to him, "Go to the shop of . . . ., and get cloth for a suit for this gentleman on my account." Thereupon he turned to me and asked what sort of stuff I liked. Overpowered by a feeling of gratitude and esteem for this excellent man, I could answer nothing. The tears streaming down my cheeks served for my only answer.

The chief rabbi also ordered new linen for me. In two days everything was ready. Dressed in my new linen and new suit, I went to the chief rabbi. I was going to express my gratitude to him, but could scarcely get out a few broken words. For the chief rabbi this was a charming sight. He waived my thanks, and said that I was not to think too highly of him for this, inasmuch as what he had done was a mere trifle not worth mentioning.

Now the reader may perhaps suppose that this chief rabbi was a wealthy man, for whom the expense to which he put himself on my account was really a trifle; but I can assure him that this was far from being the case. He had merely a moderate income; and as he occupied himself wholly with study, his wife had the management of his affairs, and especially the charge of housekeeping. Actions of this sort, therefore, had to be done without the knowledge of his wife, and under the pretext that he received money for the purpose from other people. Moreover, he lived a very temperate life, fasted every day except Sabbath, and never ate flesh the whole week through. Nevertheless, to satisfy his benevolent inclinations, he could not avoid making debts. His austere manner of life, his many studies and vigils, weakened his strength to such a degree that he died about the thirty-sixth year of his life. His death took place after he had been appointed chief rabbi in Fördet, to which place he was followed by a large number of disciples. I can never think of this godly man without being deeply affected.

In my former lodging at the poor tailor's I had left some trifles which I now went to fetch. The tailor, his wife, and my former comrade in beggary, who had already heard of the happy change in my affairs, expected me with the greatest impatience. It was a touching scene. The man, who three days before arrived in this poor hut, quite debilitated, half-naked, and barefoot, whom the poor inmates of the house regarded as an outcast of nature, and whose comrade in linen blouse had looked down upon him with mockery and contempt—this man (his fame before him) now comes into the same hut with a cheerful face, and in the decent garb of a chief rabbi.

They all testified their joy and surprise at the transformation. The poor woman took her babe in her arms and, with tears in her eyes, begged a blessing for him. My comrade touchingly begged me for forgiveness on account of his rough treatment. He said that he deemed himself fortunate in having had such a fellow traveler, but would hold himself unfortunate if I would not forgive the faults he had committed in ignorance. I spoke to them all very kindly, gave the little one my blessing, handed my old comrade all the cash I had in my pocket, and went back deeply affected.

Meanwhile my fame was spread through the whole town by the chief rabbi's attitude towards me, as well as that of my new host, who was himself a scholar and had formed a high opinion of my talents and learning from our frequent conversations and discussions. All the scholars of the town came to see me and discuss with me as a famous traveling rabbi; and the more intimately they came to know me, the higher their esteem rose.

This period was undoubtedly the happiest and most honorable in my life. The young scholars of the town passed a resolution at their meeting to make up a salary for me, in return for which I was to deliver lectures to them on the celebrated and profound work of Maimonides, *Moreh Nebukhim*. But this proposal was never carried out, because the parents of these young people were anxious lest their children should be thus led astray, and by independent thinking on religion be made to waver in their faith. They acknowledged indeed that with all my fondness for religious speculation I was still a pious man and an orthodox rabbi. But they could not rely upon their children having sufficient judgment to be able to enter upon this course without passing from one extreme to the other, from superstition to unbelief; and perhaps they were right.

After I had spent about four weeks in this way, the man with whom I lodged came to me and said, "Herr Solomon, allow me to make a proposal to you. If you are inclined merely to solitary study, you may remain here as long as you like. But if you do not wish to withdraw into such complete retirement, but are inclined to be of service to the world with your talents, there is a wealthy man here, one of the most prominent people of our town, who has an only son, and wishes nothing so much as to have you for his tutor. This man is my brother-in-law. If you will not do it for his sake, please do it for mine, and to gratify the chief rabbi, as he is deeply concerned for the education of my nephew, who is connected by marriage with his family." This offer I accepted with delight. I came therefore into this household as tutor under advantageous conditions, and remained with them two years in the greatest honor. Nothing was done in the house without my knowledge. I was always met with the greatest respect. I was in fact held to be almost something more than human.

Thus the two years flowed on imperceptibly and happily for me. But during the time some little incidents took place, which I believe should not be altogether omitted in this history. In the first place the esteem entertained for me in this house went so far that *malgré moi* they were going to make me a prophet. My pupil was betrothed to the daughter of a chief rabbi, who was a brother-in-law of the chief rabbi in Posen. The bride, a girl of about twelve years, was brought to Posen by her parents-in-law at the feast of Pentecost. On the occasion of this visit I observed that the girl was of a very phlegmatic temperament and somewhat consumptive. I mentioned this to the brother of my host, and added, with a significant look, that I was very anxious for the girl, as I did not believe that her health would last long. After the feast was over the girl was sent home, and a fortnight afterwards a letter was received announcing her death. On this account, not only in the house where I lived, but in the whole town, I was taken for a prophet, who had been able to foretell the death of the girl. As I wished nothing less than to deceive, I endeavored to persuade these superstitious people otherwise. I told them that anybody who had observed the world about him could have foretold as much. But it was of no use. Once for all I was a prophet, and had to remain one.

Another incident occurred in a Jewish house one Friday when they were preparing fish for the Sabbath. The fish was a carp, and it seemed to the cook who was cutting it up as if it uttered a sound. This threw everybody into a panic. The rabbi was asked what should be done with this dumb fish that had ventured to speak. Under the superstitious idea that the carp was possessed with a spirit, the rabbi enjoined that it should be wrapped in a linen cloth and buried ceremoniously. In the house where I lived this awe-inspiring event became the subject of conversation. Having by this time emancipated myself pretty thoroughly from superstitions of this sort by diligent study of the *Moreh Nebukhim,* I laughed heartily over the story, and said that if instead of burying the carp they had sent it to me, I should have tried how such an inspired carp would taste.

This *bon mot* became known. The learned men fell into a passion about it, denounced me as a heretic, and sought to persecute me in every way. But the respect entertained for me in the house where I was tutor made all their efforts fruitless. As I found myself thus protected, the spirit of fanaticism, instead of deterring me, rather spurred me on to further reflection, and I began to push matters a little farther, frequently slept through the time of prayer, went seldom to the synagogue, and so on. At last the measure of my sins became so full that nothing could longer secure me from persecution.

At the entrance to the Communal Hall in Posen there has been, no one knows for how long, a staghorn fixed into the wall. The Jews are unanimously of the conviction that anyone who touches this horn is sure to die on the spot; and they relate a multitude of instances in proof. This would not go down with me at all, and I made fun of it. So one day, when I was passing the staghorn with some other Jews, I said to them, "You Posen fools, do you think that anyone who touches this horn must die on the spot? See, I dare to touch it!" Horror-struck, they expected my death on the spot; but as nothing happened, their anxiety for me was converted into hatred. They looked on me as one who had profaned the sanctuary.

This fanaticism stirred up in me the desire to go to Berlin, and destroy by enlightenment the remnant of superstition which still clung to me. I therefore begged leave of my employer. He politely invited me to continue in his house, and assured me of his protection against all persecution. But as I had taken my resolution, I was determined not to alter it. I therefore bade goodbye to my employer and his family, took a seat on the Frankfort post, and set out for Berlin.

CHAPTER XIX

Arrival in Berlin—Acquaintances—Mendelssohn—Desperate Study of Metaphysics—Doubts—Lectures on Locke and Adelung

THIS TIME I CAME TO BERLIN BY POST, AND SO WAS NOT required to remain outside the Rosenthaler Gate to be examined by the Jewish elders. I proceeded without any difficulty into the city, and was allowed to take up my quarters where I chose. To *remain* in the city, however, was a different matter. The Jewish police officers (L. M. of those days was a terrible fellow) made a daily circuit of the hotels and other houses designed for the reception of strangers, inquired into the quality and occupation of newcomers as well as the probable length of their stay, and allowed them no rest till they had either found some occupation in the city or were out of it again, or—the alternative is obvious. I had taken a lodging in the New Market with a Jew who was accustomed to receive poor travelers that had not much to spend, and on the following day we received a visit of this sort.

The Jewish police officer, L. M., came and examined me in the strictest manner. I told him that I wished to enter into service as a family tutor in Berlin, and that the length of my stay could therefore not be precisely determined. I appeared suspicious to him; he believed he had seen me before, and evidently looked on me as a comet which comes nearer earth the second time than the first and so makes the danger more threatening. But when he saw I had a *Millot ha-Higgayon,* or Hebrew Logic, composed by Maimonides and annotated by Mendelssohn, he went into a perfect rage. "Yes! yes!" he exclaimed, "that's the sort of book!" He turned to me with a threatening look and said, "Pack! out of Berlin as quick as you can, if you don't wish to be led out with an escort!" I trembled and knew not what to do; but as I had learned that there was a Polish Jew residing in Berlin for the sake of study, a man of talent, and received in the best houses, I paid him a visit.

He received me as a countryman in a very friendly manner, asked about my home in Poland, and what had brought me to Berlin. I told him in reply that from my childhood I had discovered an inclination to the sciences, had already made myself acquainted with this and that Hebrew work which touches upon them, and now had come to Berlin in order to be *maamik behokhmah* (to become absorbed in the sciences). He smiled at this quaint rabbinical phrase, but gave me his full approval; and after conversing with me for some time, he begged me to visit him often, which I very willingly promised to do, and went away rejoicing in spirit.

The very next day I visited my Polish friend again,

and found with him some young people belonging to a prominent Jewish family, who visited him often and conversed with him on scientific subjects. They entered into conversation with me, found much amusement in my jargon, as well as in my simplicity and openheartedness; in particular they laughed heartily at the phrase, *maamik behokhmah,* of which they had already heard. All this gave me courage, and they assured me that I should not find myself mistaken in the expectation of being able to be *maamik behokhmah* in Berlin. And when I made known my fear of the police officer, they bade me pluck up courage and promised to obtain protection for me from their family, so that I might remain in Berlin as long as I chose.

As I now had permission to remain in Berlin, I thought of nothing but how to carry my purpose into effect. By chance I went into a butter shop one day, and found the dealer in the act of anatomizing a somewhat old book for use in his trade. I looked at it and found, to my no small astonishment, that it was Wolff's *Metaphysics, or the Doctrine of God, of the World, and of Man's Soul.* I could not understand how in a city so enlightened as Berlin such important works could be treated in this barbarous fashion. I turned to the dealer, and asked if he would not sell the book. He was ready to part with it for two groschen. Without thinking long about it I paid the price at once, and went home delighted with my treasure.

At the very first reading I was in raptures with the book. Not only this sublime science in itself, but also the order and mathematical method of the celebrated author—the precision of his explanations, the exactness of his reasoning, and the scientific arrangement of his exposition—all this gave my mind quite a new light.

In the Ontology, the Cosmology, and the Psychology, I got on well enough but I found the Theology perplexing, for its dogmas were not only not in harmony with, but even contradictory to, the preceding propositions. At the very beginning I could not assent to Wolff's argument *a posteriori* for the existence of God in accordance with the Principle of Sufficient Reason. I objected that, since by Wolff's own confession, the Principle of Sufficient Reason is abstracted from particular cases of experience, all that it can prove is, that every object of experience must have its sufficient reason in some other object of experience, but not in an object beyond all experience. I also compared these new metaphysical doctrines with those of Maimonides, or rather of Aristotle, which were already known to me; and I could not reconcile them.

I therefore resolved to set these doubts forth in Hebrew and to send what I wrote to Herr Mendelssohn, of whom I had already heard so much. When he received my communication, he was not a little astonished at it. He replied at once that my doubts were in fact well-founded, that I should nevertheless not allow them to discourage me, but continue to study with the zeal with which I had begun.

Thus encouraged, I wrote a Hebrew dissertation in which I questioned the foundations of Revealed as well as of Natural Theology. All the thirteen articles of faith laid down by Maimonides, I attacked with philosophical arguments, with the exception of one, namely that on reward and punishment, to which I conceded philosophical relevance as the necessary consequence of free will. I sent this dissertation to Mendelssohn, who was quite amazed that a Polish Jew who had scarcely got as far as seeing Wolff's *Metaphysics* was so soon able to penetrate into their depths to the point of questioning their conclusions by means of a correct Ontology. He invited me to call, and I accepted his invitation. But I was shy, and the manners and customs of the Berliners were strange to me, and it was with trepidation and embarrassment that I ventured to enter a fashionable house. When I opened Mendelssohn's door, and saw him and other gentlefolk there, as well as the beautiful rooms and elegant furniture, I shrank back, closed the door, and had a mind not to go in. But Mendelssohn had noticed me. He came out and spoke to me very kindly, led me into his room, placed himself beside me at the window, and paid me many compliments about my writing. He assured me that if I persisted, I should in a short time make great progress in Metaphysics; and he promised to resolve my doubts. Not satisfied with this, the worthy man looked after my maintenance also, recommended me to the most eminent, enlightened, and wealthy Jews of Berlin, who made provision for my board and other wants. I was given the freedom of their tables, and their libraries were open to my use.

Especially worthy of mention among these gentlemen was H...., a man of many attainments and excellent disposition, who was a particular friend and disciple of Mendelssohn. He took great pleasure in my conversation, and we often discussed profound subjects in Natural Theology and Morals, on which I expressed my thoughts to him quite frankly and without disguise. In the way of conversation I touched upon the various systems known to me that are generally denounced, and stubbornly defended them. He adduced objections; I answered them, and objected in turn to the opposing systems. At first this friend regarded me as a speaking animal, and entertained himself with me as one might with a dog or a starling that has been taught to pronounce a few words. The odd mixture of the animal in my manners, my expressions, and my whole outward behavior, with the rational in my thoughts, excited his imagination more than the subject of our conversation roused his understanding. By degrees the fun was turned to earnest. He began to give his attention to the subjects themselves. But notwithstanding his other capabilities and attainments, he had no head for philosophy and the liveliness of his imagination generally interfered with the soundness of his judgment. The results of our conversations may be readily imagined.

Herr A.... M.... also, a good, honest fellow, and at that time wealthy, allowed me free access to his house. Here I found Locke in the German translation, and I was pleased with him at the first hasty glance, for I recognized him as the best of the modern philosophers, a man concerned only with truth. I offered the tutor of Herr A.... M....'s household instruction on this admirable work. At first he smiled at my simplicity in proposing that I, who had scarcely got the length of seeing Locke, should give lessons to him, whose native tongue was German and who had been brought up in the sciences. But he behaved as if he found nothing offensive, accepted my proposal, and fixed an hour for the lessons. I presented myself at the time appointed, and began the lessons; but as I could not read a word of German correctly, I told my pupil to read the text aloud paragraph by paragraph, and I would expound each paragraph to him. My pupil, who pretended to be in earnest, consented to this also, to carry on the joke; but how great was his astonishment when he found that there was to be no joke and that my expositions and remarks, though delivered in my own peculiar language, in fact evinced a genuine philosophical spirit.

It was still more amusing when I became acquainted with the family of Widow Levi, and made the proposal to her son, the young Herr Samuel Levi, who is still my Maecenas, that he should take lessons from me in the German language. The studious youth, incited by my reputation, was resolved to make a trial, and wished me to explain Adelung's *German Grammar*. I had never seen Adelung's grammar, but would not allow myself to be disconcerted on that account. (The method by which I had learned to read and to understand books without any preparatory studies, and to which I had been driven in Poland by the want of books, grew to such an expertness that I felt certain beforehand of being able to understand anything.) My pupil was obliged to read Adelung bit by bit, while I not only expounded it, but added glosses of my own. In particular, I found a good deal to take exception to in Adelung's philosophical explanation of the parts of speech; and I drew up an explanation of my own, which I communicated to my intelligent pupil, by whom it is still preserved.

As a man altogether without experience I carried my frankness a little too far at times, and brought upon myself many vexations in consequence.

CHAPTER XX

Departure from Berlin—Sojourn in Hamburg and Amsterdam —A Silly Old Woman Falls in Love with Me, but Is Rejected

I FOUND GRATIFICATION NOT ONLY IN THE STUDY OF THE sciences, but generally in everything good and beautiful which came my way; and my enthusiasm was boundless. An inclination to the pleasures of the senses, hitherto suppressed, also asserted its claims. The first occasion for such enjoyment came about as follows: For many years certain men who were occupied in various kinds of teaching had insinuated themselves into the most prominent and wealthy Jewish families of Berlin. They devoted themselves especially to the French language (which was then regarded as the highest point of enlightenment), to geography, arithmetic, bookkeeping, and similar studies. They had also made themselves familiar with some phrases and imperfectly understood conclusions of the more profound sciences and philosophical systems, while their intercourse with the fair sex was marked by studious gallantry. As a result of all this, they were great favorites in the families where they visited, and were regarded as clever fellows. Now they began to observe that my reputation was always on the increase and that the respect for my attainments and talents had so grown that they were being quite eclipsed. Accordingly, they contrived a stratagem, whereby they might ward off the threatening danger.

They invited me into their society, protested their friendship and esteem for me, and begged the honor of my company. Suspecting no harm, I received their advances with pleasure, especially as I reflected that Mendelssohn and my other friends were too grand for everyday intercourse with me. It seemed to me very desirable to find some friends of a middle station with whom I could associate *sans façon* and enjoy the charms of familiarity. My new friends took me into gay society, to taverns, on pleasure excursions, at last also to . . . . ; and all this at their own expense. For my part I cheerfully laid bare all the mysteries of philosophy, explained the details of the disparate systems, and corrected their notions on various subjects of human knowledge. But as things of this sort cannot be poured into a man's head, and as these gentlemen had no special capacity for them, of course they were not able to make any great progress by this kind of instruction. When I observed this I began to show a sort of contempt for them, and made no attempt to conceal the fact that it was mainly the roast and the wine that gave me pleasure in their company. This did not please them particularly; and as they were unable to reach their object with me completely, they tried to reach it at least in part. They told tales to my grand friends behind my back about the most trifling incidents and expressions. For instance, they asserted that I charged Mendelssohn with being a philosophical hypocrite, that I declared others to be shallow, that I was seeking to spread dangerous systems, and that I was wholly abandoned to Epicureanism (as if they were genuine Stoics!). At last they even began to manifest their enmity openly.

All this, of course, had its effect; and to add to the unfavorable impression, my friends observed that in my studies I pursued no fixed plan, but merely followed my inclination. Accordingly, they proposed to me that I should study medicine, but could not induce me to do it.

Eventually it was proposed that I study pharmacy; and as I had already obtained some acquaintance with physics, as well as chemistry, I consented. My object, however, was not to make practical use of my attainments, but merely to acquire theoretical knowledge. Accordingly, instead of setting to with my own hands and so acquiring expertness, I played the part of a mere spectator at important chemical demonstrations. In this way I learned pharmacy, yet without being able to become an apothecary. After the lapse of a three years' apprenticeship, Madame Rosen, in whose shop I was apprenticed, was duly paid by H.J.D. the promised fee of sixty thalers. I received a certificate attesting that I had perfectly mastered the art of pharmacy; and so the whole matter ended with everything correct.

But all this helped alienate my friends. At last Mendelssohn asked me to come and see him, whereupon he informed me of their alienation, and pointed out its causes. They complained, firstly, that I had not made up my mind to any plan of life, and had thereby rendered fruitless all their exertions in my behalf; secondly, that I was trying to spread dangerous opinions and systems; and thirdly, that I was rumored to be leading a loose life, and to be much addicted to sensual pleasures.

The first of these complaints I endeavored to answer by referring to the fact, which I had mentioned to my friends at the very first, that in consequence of my peculiar upbringing, I was not suited for any kind of business but only for a quiet speculative life. Following such a life I could not only satisfy my natural inclination, but by teaching and similar means maintain myself after a fashion. "As to the second point," I proceeded, "the opinions and systems referred to are either true or false. If the former, then I do not see how the knowledge of the truth can do any harm. If the latter, then let them be refuted. Moreover, I have explained these opinions and systems only to gentlemen who desire to be enlightened, and to rise above prejudices. But the truth is that it is not the mischievous nature of the opinions but the incapacity of those gentlemen to comprehend them, coupled with their reluctance to make such a humiliating confession, that sets them in arms against me. In reference to the third reproach, I must say with downright honesty, Herr Mendelssohn, we are all Epicureans. The moralists can prescribe to us merely rules of prudence; that is to say, they can prescribe the use of means for the attainment of given ends, but not the ends themselves." "But," I added, "I see clearly that I must quit Berlin; whither, is a matter of indifference." With this I bade Mendelssohn farewell. He gave me a very favorable testimonial of my capabilities and talents, and wished me a prosperous journey. Samuel Levi also gave me a letter of introduction to one of his correspondents in Hamburg.

When I arrived in Hamburg, I went to the merchant to whom this letter was addressed, and delivered it. He received me well, and invited me to his table during my stay in the city. But as he knew nothing except how to make money, and took no particular interest in scholarship or science, he evidently entertained me merely on account of my letter of introduction, because he had to do something to gratify his correspondent. As I knew nothing of trade and besides made no very presentable figure, he endeavored to be rid of me as soon as possible, and to that end asked me where I meant to go when I left Hamburg. When I replied that I was going to Holland, he gave me the kindly advice to hasten my departure, as this was the best season of the year for traveling. Accordingly, I took out a passage on a Hamburg vessel that was to sail for Holland in two or three weeks. At last we got a favorable wind, the vessel stood out to sea, and on the third day after our departure we arrived at Amsterdam, where I landed.

I had no acquaintances here, and as I knew that there was a gentleman belonging to a prominent Berlin family at The Hague, and that he had engaged a tutor from Berlin with whom I was acquainted, I set out for that place in a canal barge.

At The Hague I took lodgings at the house of a poor Jewish woman. Before I had time to rest from my journey, a man of tall, spare figure, in untidy clothing, and with a pipe in his mouth, came in, and without observing me commenced to speak with my landlady. At last she said to him, "Herr H...., here is a stranger from Berlin; pray speak to him." The man thereupon turned to me, and asked me who I was. With my usual native frankness and candor, I told him that I was born in Poland, that my love of the sciences had induced me to spend some years in Berlin, and that now I had come to Holland with the intention of entering some employment if opportunity offered. When he heard that I was a man of learning, he began to speak with me on various subjects in philosophy, and especially in mathematics, in which he had done a good deal. He found in me a man after his own heart, and we at once formed a bond of mutual friendship.

I now went to seek the tutor from Berlin, of whom I have spoken. He introduced me to his employer as a man of high talent who had attracted much attention in Berlin and had brought letters of introduction from that city. This gentleman, who made much of his tutor as well as of everything that came from Berlin, invited me to dinner. As my external appearance did not appear to promise much, and I was besides thoroughly exhausted and depressed by my sea voyage, I cut a comical figure at table, and our host evidently did not know what to think of me. But as he put great confidence in the written recommendation of Mendelssohn and the oral recommendation of his tutor, he suppressed his astonishment, and invited me to his table as long as I chose to remain in The Hague. In the evening he invited his brothers-in-law to meet me. They were sons of B...., celebrated for his wealth as well as his beneficence; and as they were themselves scholars, they were expected to sound me out. They conversed with me on various subjects in the Talmud, and even in the Kabbalah. When I showed myself thoroughly initiated into the mysteries of this sort of learning, even explained to them passages which they regarded as inexplicable, and unravelled the most complicated knots of argument, their admiration was aroused, and they believed they had come upon a great man.

It was not long, however, before their admiration turned into hatred. The occasion for the change was as follows: In connection with the Kabbalah, they told me of a godly man who had long resided in London and who was able to perform miracles by means of the Kabbalah. I expressed some doubts, but they assured me they had been present at performances of the kind during this man's residence at The Hague. To this I replied as a philosopher that I did not indeed question the truth of their statement, but that perhaps they had not duly investigated the matter themselves, and had presented their preconceived opinions as facts. Moreover, I declared that I must regard the effect of the Kabbalah in general with scepticism, until it is shown that that effect is of such a kind as cannot be explained in accordance with the known laws of Nature. This declaration they held to be heresy.

At the close of the meal the wine cup was passed to me, that I might pronounce the blessing over it, as custom required. I declined the honor with the explanation that I did so not from any false shame of speaking before a gathering, because in Poland I had been a rabbi and had very often held disputations and delivered sermons before large assemblies; to prove this I offered to deliver public lectures daily. It was only love of truth, I declared, and reluctance to be guilty of inconsistency, that made it impossible for me, without manifest aversion, to say prayers which I regarded as a result of an anthropomorphic system of theology.

At this their patience was completely exhausted; they reviled me as a damnable heretic, and declared it would be a deadly sin to tolerate me in a Jewish house. Our host, who was no philosopher indeed, but a reasonable and enlightened man, did not much mind what they said; my humble talents were of more value in his eyes than my piety. Accordingly, they broke up immediately after dinner, and left the house in deep displeasure; but all their subsequent efforts to drive me from their brother-in-law's house were fruitless. I remained in it about nine months, lived at perfect freedom, but very retired, with no occupation and no rational society.

A comical scene must be mentioned here. At The Hague there lived at that time a woman of about forty-five, said to have been very pretty in her youth, who supported herself by giving lessons in French. One day she called upon me at my lodging, introduced herself, and expressed an irresistible yearning for scientific conversation. She declared that she would visit me at my lodging often, and requested the honor of a visit from me in return.

This advance I met with great pleasure, and returned her visits several times; and thus our relation became more and more intimate. We conversed usually on subjects in philosophy and *belles lettres*. I was still a married man, and, except for her enthusiasm in learning, Madam had little attraction for me, and so

I thought of nothing beyond mere entertainment. But the lady had been a widow for a pretty long while, and by her own account she conceived an affection for me. She began to express her affection by romantic looks and words, which struck me as very comical. I could never believe that a lady could fall in love with me in earnest. Her expressions of affection, therefore, I took for mere affectation. But she showed herself more and more in earnest, became thoughtful at times in the midst of our conversation, and burst into tears.

It was during a conversation of this sort that we fell upon the subject of love. I told her frankly that I could not love a woman except for the sake of womanly excellences, such as beauty, grace, agreeableness, and the like, and that any other merits she might possess, such as talents or learning, could arouse my esteem but not my love. To refute my views the lady adduced arguments *a priori*, as well as instances from experience, especially from French novels, and tried to correct my notions of love. I could not be so easily convinced; and as the lady was carrying her airs to an absurd length, I rose and took my leave. She accompanied me to the very door, grasped me by the hand, and would not let me go. I asked her somewhat sharply, "What's the matter with you, Madam?" With trembling voice and tearful eyes she replied, "I love you."

When I heard this laconic declaration of love, I began to laugh immoderately, tore myself from her grasp, and rushed away. Some time afterwards she sent me the following *billet doux*:

"Sir,

I have been greatly mistaken in your character. I took you for a man of noble thoughts and exalted feelings; but I see now that you are a genuine Epicurean. You seek nothing but pleasure. A woman can please you only on account of her beauty. A Madame Dacier, for example, who has studied thoroughly all the Greek and Latin authors, translated them into her native language, and enriched them with learned annotations, could not please you. Why? Because she is not pretty. Sir, you, who are otherwise so enlightened, ought to be ashamed to cherish such pernicious principles; and if you will not repent, then tremble before the revenge of the injured love of

Yours, etc."

To this I returned the following reply:

"Madam,

That you have been mistaken, is shown by the result. You say that I am a genuine Epicurean. In this you do me a great honor. I abhor the title of an *epicure,* but I am proud of the title of *genuine Epicurean.* Certainly it is beauty alone that pleases me in a woman; but as this can be heightened by other qualities, these must also be pleasing as means towards the chief end. On the other hand, I can merely *esteem* such a woman on account of her talents; *love* her I cannot, as I have already explained in conversation. For the learning of Madame Dacier I have all respect: she could at all events fall in love with the Greek heroes who were at the siege of Troy, and expect in return the love of their *manes* that were constantly hovering around her; but nothing more. For the rest, Madam, as far as your revenge is concerned, I do not fear it, since Time, which destroys all things, has shattered your weapons, that is, your teeth and nails.

Yours, etc."

Thus ended this strange love affair.

I discovered that in Holland there was nothing for me to do, inasmuch as the main desire of the Dutch Jews is to make money, and they manifest no particular taste for the sciences.

CHAPTER XXI

Return to Hamburg—A Lutheran Pastor Pronounces Me a Scabby Sheep, Unworthy of Admission into the Christian Fold—I Enter the Gymnasium and Frighten the Chief Rabbi out of His Wits

MY RETURN JOURNEY TO HAMBURG WAS AGREEABLE but here I fell into circumstances of the deepest distress. I lodged in a miserable house, had nothing to eat, and did not know what to do. I had grown too enlightened to return to Poland, to spend my life in misery without rational occupation or society, and to sink back into the darkness of superstition and ignorance, from which I had hardly delivered myself with so much labor. On the other hand I could not count on success in Germany owing to my ignorance of the language, as well as of the manners and customs of the people, to which I had never yet been able to adapt myself properly. I had learned no particular profession, I had not distinguished myself in any special science, I was not even master of any language in which I could make myself perfectly intelligible. It occurred to me, therefore, that for me there was no alternative left but to embrace the Christian religion and get myself baptized in Hamburg. Accordingly, I resolved to go to the first clergyman I should come upon, and inform him of my resolution, as well as of my motives for it, without hypocrisy, in a truthful and honest fashion. But as I could not express myself well orally,

I put my thoughts into writing in German with Hebrew characters, went to a schoolmaster, and got him to copy it in German characters. The purport of my letter was in brief as follows:—

"I am a native of Poland, belonging to the Jewish nation, destined by my education and studies to be a rabbi; but in the thickest darkness I have perceived some light. This induced me to search further after light and truth, and to free myself completely from the darkness of superstition and ignorance. To this end, which could not be attained in my native place, I came to Berlin, where by the support of some enlightened men of our nation I studied for some years, not indeed after any plan, but merely to satisfy my thirst for knowledge. But as our nation is unable to make use not only of such planless studies but even of those conducted on the most perfect plan, it cannot be blamed for becoming tired of them, and pronouncing their encouragement to be useless. I have therefore resolved, in order to secure temporal as well as eternal happiness, which depends on the attainment of perfection, and in order to become useful to myself as well as others, to embrace the Christian religion. The Jewish religion, it is true, comes nearer to reason in its articles of faith than Christianity. But in practical use the latter has an advantage over the former; and since morality, which consists not in opinions but in actions, is the aim of all religion in general, clearly the latter comes nearer than the former to this aim. Moreover, I hold the mysteries of the Christian religion for that which they are, that is, allegorical representations of the truths that are most important for man. By this means I make my faith in them harmonize with reason, but I cannot believe them according to their common meaning. I therefore most respectfully beg an answer to the question whether after this confession I am worthy of the Christian religion or not. In the former case, I am ready to carry my proposal into effect; but in the latter, I must give up all claim to a religion which enjoins me to lie, that is, to deliver a confession of faith which contradicts my reason."

The schoolmaster to whom I dictated this was astonished at my audacity; never before had he listened to such a confession of faith. He shook his head in perplexity, interrupted the writing several times, and wondered whether the mere copying was not itself a sin. With great reluctance he copied it out, merely to get rid of the thing. I then went to a prominent clergyman, delivered my letter, and begged for a reply. He read it with great attention, likewise showed astonishment, and on finishing entered into conversation with me.

"So," he said, "I see your intention is to embrace the Christian religion, merely in order to improve your temporal circumstances."

"Excuse me, Herr Pastor," I replied, "I think I have made it clear enough in my letter that my object is the attainment of perfection. For this, it is true, the removal of all hindrances and the improvement of my external circumstances are a prerequisite condition. But this condition is not the chief end."

"But," said the pastor, "do you not feel any inclination of the soul to the Christian religion without reference to any external motives?"

"I should be telling a lie if I were to give you an affirmative answer."

"You are too much of a philosopher," replied the pastor, "to be able to become a Christian. Reason has taken the upper hand with you, and faith must accommodate itself to reason. You hold the mysteries of the Christian religion to be mere fables, and its commands to be mere laws of reason. For the present I cannot be satisfied with your confession of faith. You should therefore pray to God, that He may enlighten you with His grace, and endow you with the spirit of true Christianity; and then come to me again."

"If that is the case," I said, "then I must confess, Herr Pastor, that I am not qualified for Christianity. Whatever light I may receive, I shall always illuminate it with the light of reason. I shall never believe that I have fallen upon new truths if it is impossible to see their connection with the truths already known to me. I must therefore remain what I am, a stiff-necked Jew. My religion enjoins me to *believe* nothing, but to *think* the truth and to *practice* goodness. If I find any hindrance in this from external circumstances, it is not my fault. I do all that lies in my power."

With this I bade the pastor goodbye.

Meanwhile a young man, who had known me in Berlin, heard of my arrival. He called on me to say that Herr W......, who had seen me in Berlin, was now residing in Hamburg, and that I might very properly call upon him. I did so, and Herr W......, who was a very clever, honorable man, of a naturally benevolent disposition, asked me what I intended to do. I represented my whole circumstances to him, and begged for his advice. He said that in his opinion the unfortunate position of my affairs arose from the fact that I had devoted myself with zeal merely to the acquisition of scientific knowledge, but had neglected the study of language and was therefore unable to communicate my knowledge to others or make any use of it. Meanwhile, he thought, nothing had been lost by delay; and if I were still willing to accommodate myself to circumstances, I could attain my object in the gymnasium in Altona, where his son was studying; he himself would provide for my support.

I accepted this offer with many thanks, and went home with a joyful heart. Meanwhile Herr W...... spoke to the professors of the gymnasium, as well as to the principal, but more particularly to the syndic, Herr G......, a man who cannot be sufficiently praised. He represented to them that I was a man of uncommon talents who wanted merely some further knowledge of language to distinguish himself in the world, and who hoped to obtain that knowledge by a short residence in the gymnasium. They acceded to his request. I was matriculated, and had a lodging assigned me in the institution.

Here I lived several years in peace and contentment. But the pupils in such a gymnasium, as may be supposed, make very slow progress; and it was therefore natural that I, who had already made considerable attainments in science, should find the lessons at times somewhat tedious. During the whole period of my residence in the gymnasium the professors were unable to form any correct idea of me, because they never had an opportunity of getting to know me. By the end of the first year I thought I had attained my object of acquiring a good foundation in languages. I had also become tired of the inactive life, and therefore resolved to quit the gymnasium. But Director Dusch, who gradually grew acquainted with me, begged me to stay at least another year, and as I wanted for nothing I consented.

It was about this time that the following incident in my life took place. My wife had sent a Polish Jew in search of me, and he heard of my residence in Hamburg. Accordingly, he came and called on me at the gymnasium. He had been commissioned by my wife to demand that I should either return home without delay, or send a bill of divorce by his hand. At that time I was unable to do either the one or the other. I was not inclined to be divorced from my wife without cause; and to return at once to Poland, where I had not yet the slightest prospect of getting on in the world or of leading a rational life, was to me impossible. I represented all this to the gentleman who had undertaken the commission, and added that it was my intention to leave the gymnasium soon and go to Berlin. My Berlin friends, I hoped, would give me both their advice and assistance in carrying out this intention. He would not be satisfied with this answer, which he took for a mere evasion. When he found that he could do nothing with me, he went to the chief rabbi, and entered a complaint against me. A messenger was accordingly sent to summon me before the tribunal of the chief rabbi; but I took the position that I was not at present under his jurisdiction, inasmuch as the gymnasium had a jurisdiction of its own by which my case would have to be decided. The chief rabbi sought government support to make me submit to his wishes, but all his efforts were in vain. When he saw that he could not accomplish his purpose in this way, he sent me an invitation a second time, saying that he wished merely to speak with me. To this I willingly consented, and went to him at once.

He received me with much respect; and when I made known to him my birthplace and family in Poland, he began to lament and wring his hands. "Alas!" said he, "you are the son of the famous Rabbi Joshua? I know your father well; he is a pious and learned man. You also are not unknown to me; I examined you as a boy several times, and formed high expectations of you. Oh! is it possible that you have altered so?" (Here he pointed to my shaven beard.) To this

I replied that I also had the honor of knowing him, and that I still remembered his examinations well. My conduct hitherto, I told him, was as little opposed to religion properly understood, as it was to reason. "But," he interrupted, "you do not wear a beard, you do not go to the synagogue: is that not contrary to religion?" "No!" I replied, and I proved to him from the Talmud that under the circumstances in which I was placed all this was allowed. On this point we entered into a lengthy dispute, in which each maintained his right. As he could effect nothing with me by such disputation, he adopted the style of mere sermonizing; but when this also was of no avail, he began to cry aloud, *"Shofar! Shofar!"* This is the name of the horn which is blown on New Year's day as a summons to repentance, and of which it is supposed that Satan is horribly afraid. While the chief rabbi called out the word, he pointed to a *shofar* that lay before him on the table, and asked me, "Do you know what that is?" I replied, quite boldly, "Oh yes! it is a ram's horn." At these words the chief rabbi fell back upon his chair, and began to lament over my lost soul. I left him to lament as long as he liked, and bade him goodbye.

At the end of my second year I began to reflect that it would favor my future success as well as be fair to the gymnasium if I should make myself better known to the professors. Accordingly, I went to Director Dusch, announced to him that I was soon to leave, and told him that as I wished a certificate from him, it would be well for him to examine me on the progress I had made, so that this certificate might correspond to the truth. To this end he had me translate some passages from Latin and English works in prose as well as in verse, and was very well pleased with the translation. Afterwards, he entered into conversation with me on some subjects in philosophy, but found me so well versed in these, that he was obliged to retreat for his own safety. At last he asked me, "But how is it with your mathematics?" I begged him to examine me in this also. "In our mathematical lessons," he began, "we had advanced to somewhere about the subject of solids. Will you work out yourself a proposition not yet taken up in the lessons, for example, that about the relation of the cylinder, the sphere, and the cone to one another? You may take some days to do it." I replied that this was unnecessary, and offered to perform the task on the spot. I then demonstrated not only the proposition prescribed, but several others out of Segner's *Geometry*. The director was much surprised, called all the pupils in the gymnasium, and represented to them that the extraordinary progress I had made should make them ashamed of themselves. Most of them did not know what to say to this; but some replied, "Do not suppose, Herr Director, that Maimon made this progress in mathematics here. He has seldom attended the mathematical lessons, and even when he was there he paid no attention." They were going to say more, but the Director commanded silence, and gave me an honorable certificate, which became a constant spur to higher attainments.

I now bade goodbye to the teachers and officers of the gymnasium, who all complimented me by saying I had done honor to their institution. I then set out once more for Berlin.

CHAPTER XXII

Third Journey to Berlin—Frustrated Plan of Hebrew Authorship
—Journey to Breslau—Divorce

ON MY ARRIVAL IN BERLIN I CALLED UPON MENDELS-
sohn, as well as other old friends, and asked them, as I
had now acquired some knowledge of languages, to
employ me in some occupation suited to my capacity.
They hit upon the suggestion that, in order to enlighten the Polish Jews still living in darkness, I should
prepare in Hebrew, as the only language intelligible
to them, some scientific works, which these philanthro-
pists would then print at their own expense, and dis-
tribute among the people. This proposal I accepted
with alacrity. But now the question arose, with what
sort of works should a beginning be made? On this
point my excellent friends were divided in their opinions. One thought that the history of the Jewish nation
would be most serviceable for the purpose, inasmuch
as the people would discover in it the origin of their
religious doctrines and of the subsequent corruption
which these had undergone. They would also come to
understand that the fall of the Jewish state, as well as
all the subsequent persecution and oppression which
the Jews had suffered, had arisen from their own ignorance and opposition to all rational planning.
Accordingly, this gentleman recommended that I
translate Basnage's *History of the Jews* from the
French. He provided me with the book and asked me
to submit a specimen of my translation. The specimen
gave satisfaction to them all, even to Mendelssohn,
and I was ready to take the work in hand. But one of
our friends thought that we ought to begin with something on natural religion and rational morality, inasmuch as this is the object of all enlightenment. Ac-

cordingly, he recommended that for this purpose I translate the *Natural Religion* of Reimarus. Mendelssohn withheld his opinion, because he believed that whatever was undertaken in this line, though it would do no harm, would also be of little use. I myself undertook these works, not from any conviction of my own, but at the requests of my friends.

Without fixing a definite plan for my labors, my friends resolved to send me to Dessau, where I could carry on my work at leisure.

I reached Dessau, hoping that after a few days my friends in Berlin would reach some definite decision, but in this I was deceived, for as soon as I turned my back on Berlin, nothing further was done about the plan. I waited about a fortnight, and when I still received no communication, I wrote to Berlin in the following terms: "If my friends cannot unite upon a plan, they might leave the settlement of it to my own judgment. For my part, I believe that to enlighten the Jewish people, we must begin neither with history nor with natural theology and morals. One of my reasons for thinking so is that these subjects, being easily intelligible, are not adapted to instil regard for science in general among the more learned Jews, who are accustomed to respect only those studies which involve a strain upon the highest intellectual powers. But a second reason is that the subjects would frequently conflict with religious prejudices, and so would never be admitted. Besides, properly speaking, there is no history of the Jewish people, for they have scarcely ever stood in political relation with other civilized nations. With the exception of the Old Testament, Josephus, and a few fragments on the persecutions of the Jews in the Middle Ages, nothing is to be found recorded on the subject. I believe, therefore, that it

97

would be best to make a beginning with some science which, besides being most favorable for the development of the mind, is also self-evident, and stands in no connection with any religious opinions. Of this sort are the mathematical sciences; and therefore with this object in view I am willing to write a mathematical textbook in Hebrew."

To this I received the answer that I might follow my plan. Accordingly, I applied myself with all diligence to the preparation of this textbook, using the Latin work on mathematics by Wolff as a basis; and in two months it was finished. I then returned to Berlin to give an account of my work, but immediately received from one of the interested gentlemen the disappointing information that, as the work was very voluminous and would entail heavy expenditure, especially on account of the copperplates required, he could not undertake the publication at his own expense; I might therefore do with my manuscript whatever I chose. I complained to Mendelssohn; and he thought that it was certainly unreasonable to let my work go without remuneration, but that I could not require my friends to undertake the publication of a work which could not be expected to produce effective results in consequence of that aversion to all science which I myself knew to be prevalent among the Jewish people. His advice, therefore, was that I should get the book printed by subscription. With this I must needs content myself. Mendelssohn and the other enlightened Jews in Berlin subscribed. For my pains I received only my manuscript and the list of subscriptions. The whole plan received no further attention.

On this I again fell out with my friends in Berlin. In this dispute Mendelssohn remained neutral, because he thought that both parties had right on their side. He promised to use his influence to induce my friends to provide for my subsistence in some other way. But when even this was not done, I became impatient, and resolved to quit Berlin once more, and go to Breslau. I took with me some letters of introduction, but they were of little service; for before I reached Breslau myself, letters in the spirit of those which Uriah carried had preceded me, and left a bad impression with most of those to whom my letters of introduction were addressed. Naturally, I was coldly received; and as I knew nothing of the later letters, I found it impossible to explain my reception, and had made up my mind to quit Breslau.

Irritated by my disheartening situation, I resolved to form the acquaintance of Christian scholars, by whose recommendation I thought I might find a hearing among the wealthy men of my own people. I could not but fear, however, that my defective language might form an obstacle to the expression of my thoughts; so I prepared a written essay, in which I recorded my ideas on the most important questions of philosophy, in the form of aphorisms. With this essay I went to the celebrated Professor Garve, explained my intention briefly, and submitted my aphorisms for examination. He discussed them with me in a very friendly manner, gave me a good testimonial, and also recommended me orally in very emphatic terms to the wealthy banker, Lipmann Meier. The gentleman settled a monthly allowance on me for my support, and also spoke to some other Jews on the subject.

My situation now improved every day. Many young men of the Jewish people sought my society. Among others, the second son of Herr Aaron Zadig took so much pleasure in my humble personality that he desired to enjoy my instruction in the sciences. This he earnestly begged his father to allow; and the latter, being a well-to-do, enlightened man of great good sense, who wished to give his children the best German education and spared no expense for that object, willingly gave his consent. He sent for me, and made the proposal that I should live at his house, and for a moderate honorarium should give his second son lessons for two hours a day in physics and *belles lettres,* and also a lesson in arithmetic of an hour a day to his third and youngest son. This proposal I accepted with great willingness.

In this house I was able to carry on but little study for myself. In the first place, there was a want of books, and, in the second place, I lived in a room with the children, where they were occupied with other matter every hour of the day. Besides, the liveliness of these young people did not suit my character which had already become somewhat austere; and therefore often had occasion to be annoyed by petty outbursts of unruliness. Consequently, as I was obliged to pass most of my time in idleness, I sought society. I often visited Herr Heimann Lisse, a plump little man of enlightened mind and cheerful disposition. With him and some other jolly companions, I spent my evenings in talk and jest and play of every sort. During the day I strolled about among the coffee houses.

I soon became acquainted in other families also particularly in those of Herr Simon, the banker, and Herr Bortenstein, both of whom showed me much kindness. All sought to persuade me to devote myself to medicine, for which I had always entertained great dislike. But when I saw from my circumstances that it would be difficult for me to find support in any other way, I allowed myself to be persuaded. Professor Garve introduced me to Professor Morgenbesser, and

I attended his medical lectures for some time. But after all I could not overcome my dislike for the art, and accordingly gave up the lectures. By and by I became acquainted with other Christian scholars, especially with the late Herr Lieberkühn, who was so justly esteemed on account of his abilities as well as for his warm interest in the welfare of mankind. I also made the acquaintance of some teachers of merit in the Jesuits' College at Breslau.

At last my situation in Breslau also grew precarious. The children of Herr Zadig, in pursuance of the occupations to which they were destined in life, entered into commercial situations, and therefore required teachers no longer. Other means of support also gradually failed. As I was thus obliged to seek subsistence in some other way, I devoted myself to giving lessons. I taught Euler's *Algebra* to a young man, gave two children instruction in the rudiments of German and Latin, and had other pupils. But even this did not last long, and I found myself in a sorrowful plight.

Meanwhile, my wife and eldest son arrived from Poland. A woman of rude education and manners but of great good sense and the courage of an Amazon, she demanded that I should at once return home with her, not seeing that what she asked was impossible. I had now lived in Germany some years, had happily emancipated myself from the fetters of superstition and religious prejudice, had abandoned the rude manner of life in which I had been brought up, and had extended my knowledge in many directions. I could not return to my former barbarous and miserable condition, deprive myself of all the advantages I had gained, and expose myself to rabbinical rage at the slightest deviation from the ceremonial law or the utterance of a liberal opinion. I represented to her that I could not go at once, that I should require first of all to make my situation known to my friends here as well as in Berlin and solicit from them the assistance of two or three hundred thalers, so that I might be able to live in Poland independent of my religious associates. But she would listen to nothing of all this, and declared her resolution to obtain a divorce if I would not go with her immediately. I could only choose the lesser of two evils, and I consented to the divorce.

Meanwhile, however, I was obliged to provide for the lodging and board of these guests, and to introduce them to my friends in Breslau. Both of these duties I performed, and I pointed out, especially to my son, the difference between the manner of life one leads here and that in Poland. I sought to convince my son by several passages in the *Moreh Nebukhim* that enlightenment of the understanding and refinement of manners are rather favorable to religion than otherwise. I went further, and sought to convince him that he ought to remain with me. I assured him that with my direction and the support of my friends he would find opportunities of developing the good abilities with which Nature had endowed him, and would obtain for them some suitable employment. These representations made some impression upon him; but my wife went with my son to consult some orthodox Jew in whose advice she thought she could thoroughly confide, and they urged her to press at once for a divorce, and on no account to let my son be induced to remain with me. This resolution, however, she was not to disclose till she had received from me a sufficient sum of money for household purposes. She might then separate from me forever, and start for home with her booty.

This pretty plan was faithfully followed. By and by I had succeeded in collecting some score of ducats from my friends. I gave them to my wife, and explained to her that to complete the required sum it would be necessary for us to go to Berlin. She then began to raise difficulties and declared point-blank that for us a divorce was best, as neither could I live happily with her in Poland, nor she with me in Germany. In my opinion she was perfectly right. But it still made me sorry to lose a wife for whom I had once entertained affection, and I could not let the affair be dealt with lightheartedly. I told her, therefore, that I should consent to a divorce only if it were enjoined by the courts.

This was done. I was summoned before the court. My wife stated the grounds on which she claimed a divorce. The president of the court then said, "Under these circumstances we can do nothing but advise a divorce." "Herr President," I replied, "we came here, not to ask advice, but to receive a judicial sentence." Thereupon the chief rabbi rose from his seat (that what he said might not have the force of a judicial decision), approached me with the codex in his hand, and pointed to the following passage: "A vagabond who abandons his wife for years, and does not write to her or send her money, shall, when he is found, be obliged to grant a divorce." "It is not my part," I replied, "to institute a comparison between this case and mine. That duty falls to you, as judge. Take your seat again, therefore, and pronounce your judicial sentence on the case."

The president became pale and red by turns, rose and sat down again, while the rest of the judges looked at one another. At last the presiding judge became furious, began to call me names, pronounced me a damnable heretic, and cursed me in the name of the

Lord. I left him to storm, however, and went away. Thus ended this strange suit, and things remained as they were before.

My wife now saw that nothing was to be done by means of force, and therefore she took to entreaty. I also yielded at last, but only on condition that at the judicial divorce the judge who had shown himself such a master of cursing should not preside in the court. After the divorce my wife returned to Poland with my son. I remained in Breslau for some time; but as my circumstances became worse and worse, I resolved to return to Berlin.

CHAPTER XXIII

Fourth Journey to Berlin—Unfortunate Circumstances—Help—Study of Kant's Writings—My Own Works

WHEN I CAME TO BERLIN, MENDELSSOHN WAS NO LONGER alive, and my former friends were determined to know nothing more of me. I did not know what to do. In the greatest distress I received a visit from Herr Bendavid, who told me that he had heard of my unfortunate circumstances, and had collected a small sum of about thirty thalers, which he gave to me. Besides, he introduced me to a Herr Jojard, an enlightened and high-minded man, who received me in a very friendly manner, and made some provision for my support. A certain professor, indeed, tried to do me an ill turn with this worthy man by denouncing me as an atheist; but in spite of this I gradually got on so well, that I was able to hire a lodging in a garret from an old woman.

I had now resolved to study Kant's *Critique of Pure Reason*, of which I had often heard but which I had never yet seen. The method by which I studied this work was quite peculiar. On the first perusal I obtained a vague idea of each section. This I afterwards endeavored to make distinct by my own reflection, and thus to penetrate into the author's meaning. Such is properly the process which is called *thinking oneself into a system*. But as I had already mastered the systems of Spinoza, Hume and Leibnitz in this way, I was naturally led to think of a system that would synthesize them all. This in fact I found, and I gradually put it in writing in the form of explanatory observations on the *Critique of Pure Reason,* just as this system unfolded itself to my mind. Such was the origin of my *Transcendental Philosophy*.

When I had finished this work, I showed it to Marcus Herz.[1] He acknowledged that he was reckoned among the most eminent disciples of Kant and had applied himself assiduously while attending Kant's philosophical lectures, as may indeed be seen from his writings, but that he was not yet in a position to pass judgment on the *Critique* itself or on any work relating to it. He advised me, however, to send my manuscript directly to Kant himself, and submit it to his judgment, and promised to accompany it with a letter to the great philosopher. Accordingly, I wrote to Kant, sending him my work and enclosing the letter from Herz. A good while passed before an answer came. At length Herz received a reply, in which, among other things, Kant said:

"But what were you thinking about, my dear friend, when you sent me a big packet containing the most subtle researches, not only to read through, but to think out thoroughly, while I am still, in my sixty-

[1] Marcus Herz, philosophical Jewish physician of Berlin, 1747-1803.

sixth year, burdened with a vast amount of labor in the completion of my plan! Part of this labor is to finish the last part of the *Critique,* namely, that on the Faculty of Judgment, which is soon to appear; part is to work out my system of the Metaphysic of Nature, as well as the Metaphysic of Ethics, in accordance with the requirements of the *Critique*. Moreover, I am kept incessantly busy with a multitude of letters requiring special explanations on particular points; and in addition to all this, my health is frail. I had already made up my mind to send back the manuscript with an excuse so well justified on all these grounds; but a glance at it soon enabled me to recognize its merits, and showed not only that none of my opponents had understood me and the main problem so well, but that very few could claim so much penetration as Herr Maimon in profound inquiries of this sort. This induced me . . ." and so on.

In another passage of the letter Kant says: "Herr Maimon's work moreover contains so many acute observations that he cannot give it to the public without its producing an impression strongly in his favor." In a letter to myself he said: "Your esteemed request I have endeavored to comply with as far as was possible for me; and if I have not gone the length of passing a judgment on the whole of your treatise, you will gather the reason from my letter to Herr Herz. Certainly it arises from no feeling of disparagement, which I entertain for no earnest effort in rational inquiries that interest mankind, and least of all for such an effort as yours, which, in point of fact, betrays no common talent for the profounder sciences."

It may easily be imagined how important and agreeable to me the approbation of this great thinker must have been, and especially his testimony that I had understood him well. For there are some arrogant Kantians who believe themselves to be sole proprietors of the Critical Philosophy, and therefore dispose of every objection, even though intended not as refutation but as fuller elaboration, by the mere baseless assertion that the author has failed to understand Kant. Now these gentlemen were no longer in a position to bring this charge against my book, inasmuch as, by the testimony of the founder of the Critical Philosophy himself, I have a better right than they to make use of this argument.

I was living in Potsdam at the time with a gentleman who was a leather manufacturer. When Kant's letters arrived, I went to Berlin, and devoted my time to the publication of my *Transcendental Philosophy*.

At this time I also began to work for the *Journal für Aufklärung*. My first article was on *Truth,* and was in the form of a letter to a friend in Berlin. The article was occasioned by a letter which I had received from this friend during my stay in Potsdam. He had written me in a humorous vein that philosophy was no longer a marketable commodity, and that I ought therefore to take advantage of the opportunity which I was enjoying to learn tanning. I replied that philosophy is not a coinage subject to the vicissitudes of the exchange; and this proposition I afterwards developed in my article. I also wrote an article on *Bacon and Kant,* in which I instituted a comparison between these two reformers of philosophy.

A number of young Jews from all parts of Germany had united, during Mendelssohn's lifetime, to form a society under the designation, *Society for Research into the Hebrew Language.* They correctly observed that the evil condition of our people, morally as well as politically, has its source in their religious prejudices, in their want of a rational exposition of the Holy Scriptures, and in the arbitrary exposition to which the rabbis are led by their ignorance of the Hebrew language. Accordingly, the object of their society was to remove these deficiencies, to study the Hebrew language at its sources, and by that means to introduce a rational exegesis. For this purpose they resolved to publish a monthly periodical in Hebrew under the title of *Hameassef* ("The Collector"),[1] which was to present expositions of difficult passages in Scripture, Hebrew poems, prose essays, translations from useful works, and the like.

The intention of all this was certainly good; but that the end would scarcely be reached by any such means, I saw from the very beginning. I was too familiar with the principles of the rabbis and their style of thought to believe that such means would bring about any change. The Jewish people is, aside from accidental modifications, a perpetual aristocracy under the appearance of a theocracy. The learned men, who form the nobility, have for many centuries been able to maintain their position as the legislative body with so much authority among the common people that they can do with them whatever they please.

I was therefore neither for nor against this monthly periodical; at times I even contributed Hebrew articles to it. Among these I will mention only one, an exposition of an obscure passage in the commentary of Maimonides on the Mishnah, which I interpreted by the Kantian philosophy. The article was afterwards translated into German, and printed in the *Berlinische Monatsschrift*.

Some time afterwards I received from this society,

[1] The periodical appeared from 1783 till 1797, first in Koenigsberg, then in Berlin, and last in Breslau.

which now styles itself the *Society for the Promotion of the Noble and Good,* a commission to write a Hebrew commentary on Maimonides' celebrated work, *Moreh Nebukhim.* This commission I undertook with pleasure, and the work was soon done. So far, however, only a part of the commentary has appeared. The preface to the work may be considered as a brief history of philosophy.

I had been an adherent of all philosophical systems in succession, Peripatetic, Spinozist, Leibnitzian, Kantian, and finally Sceptic; and I was always devoted to that system which for the time I regarded as alone true. At last I observed that all these systems contain something true, and are in certain respects equally useful. But as the differences of philosophical systems depend on the ideas which lie at their foundation in regard to the objects of nature, their properties and modifications, which cannot, like the ideas of mathematics, be defined in the same way by all men and presented *a priori,* I determined to publish for my own use, as well as for the advantage of others, a philosophical dictionary, in which all philosophical ideas should be defined according to a somewhat free method, that is, without attachment to any particular system, but either by an explanation common to all, or by several explanations from the point of view of each. Of this work also only the first part has as yet appeared.

In the popular German monthly already mentioned, the *Berlinische Monatsschrift,* various articles of mine have appeared, on Deceit, on the Power of Foreseeing, on Theodicy, and other subjects. On Empirical Psychology also I contributed various articles, and at last became associated with Herr Karl Philipp

Moritz in the editorship of the periodical *Magazin zur Erfahrungsseelenkunde.*

So much with regard to the events which have occurred in my life, and the communication of which, I thought, might be not without use. I have not yet reached the haven of rest; but

Quo nos fata trahunt retrahuntque sequamur.

EPILOGUE

Rogues whose only claim is sheer force of intellect have never been accepted by respectable society
without condescension or apology. John Addington
Symonds, Victorian England's best interpreter of
Renaissance Italy, felt constrained to explain that the
unconventional behavior which Benvenuto Cellini
professes in his autobiography is only the embroidery
of an exuberant imagination, and implied that Benvenuto himself might almost be admitted to respectable Victorian society. The foundations of Jewish respectability in an unfriendly world tend to be shaky,
and its guardians have therefore been particularly
careful to protect its brittle structure against too sharp
a knock. Before Maimon's day in Germany, and long
after it in the Russian Poland of his origin, a Jew
could achieve eminence only by religious learning,
and so there was no room for the tolerance that even
conservative society traditionally shows genius. But
roguery is itself a manifestation of human excellence,
and in certain natures it is almost the necessary ob-
verse of the coin of which mental clarity is the reverse.
In other climates people have understood this. There
is a Homeric hymn that devoutly celebrates the roguery
of Hermes, and in the Iliad Paris admonishes Hector
not to scorn the gifts of Aphrodite, for the prowess of
her protégés, too, is important in human life.

Cellini's distinction as artist and swashbuckler
came straight from his bowels, and swept away the obstacles of convention. Maimon's came from his head,
and his swashbuckling, as his distinction, took other
forms. Before the exodus from the Eastern ghetto became organized, only a resourceful and determined

man could find his way to the West, and only a singularly gifted one could win a place in the new spiritual environment. Doubtless he had as many unrecorded peers as his famous countryman the Gaon Elijah of Vilna had recorded ones. But the men who compile the records have been of the Gaon's entourage and have left no room for Maimon's type. This uniqueness of Maimon's *Autobiography* therefore enhances its interest.

In time as well as character, the *Confessions* of Jean Jacques Rousseau, who lived a generation earlier, offers a closer parallel to Maimon's *Autobiography* than does Benvenuto's. There is the same opposition to convention on the basis of reason, the same "Epicureanism" in the pursuit of sensual pleasures, the same attitude, compounded of arrogance and obsequiousness, towards patrons, the same self-dramatization, and even a similar flirting with religious conversion for expediency's sake. But Maimon's is the cleverer wit, and he has the saving grace of humor. He is more interested in spreading light (in addition to his own fame) abroad than is Jean Jacques. He is not so petulant or self-centered as Rousseau, who solemnly tells us that "Nature has destroyed the mold in which she cast me." And not so absurd, for it is simply impossible to imagine a Madame de Warens or any of her successors in Maimon's life. Maimon's intellect is both more persistent and more agile than Rousseau's. Think of a child learning astronomy by means of an armillary sphere that he had himself secretly contrived! Think of learning foreign languages from the printer's alphabet on successive signatures of bound Hebrew books! These exploits illustrate the combination of drive and imagination that Maimon applied to all his projects.

The range of his intellectual projects was as catholic, within the limits of his opportunities, as his mind was agile. Among the various interests which occupied his attention, his reputation is chiefly as a philosopher.[1] As remarkable as his work in philosophy, perhaps, is Maimon's pioneer work in experimental psychology. He collaborated in and helped edit the *Magazin zur Erfahrungsseelenkunde.*

In another field, the expert firsthand account of Jewish culture in Eastern Europe gives Maimon's *Autobiography* unique value. There the Jews has been all but crushed by a series of persecutions, and their economic situation was at its lowest. Yet the enthusiasm of even an unsympathetic observer must be aroused by the pathetic, not a little absurd, yet persistent striving for study, and the institution of a whole system of aristocracy based on degrees of achievement in learning. History shows no more gallant effort to maintain the structure of a civilized society under dehumanizing conditions. Maimon is alive to the essential gallantry, and his exasperation at the barbarism of the elementary schools and the severe limitation of the curriculum of advanced study serves only to underscore his dissatisfaction with the inefficient and dwarfing exploitation of a wholesome impulse. When his German friends planned to improve this condition by providing a series of Hebrew translations of works calculated to evangelize for a new world outlook, Maimon knew that such works would meet with resistance on their own ground. Instead, he proposed mathematics in Hebrew, trusting that mere access to a pure science

[1] A comprehensive work on Maimon's philosophy by Hugo Bergmann, in Hebrew, was published in Jerusalem in 1932. Professor Bergmann evinces high respect for Maimon's significance as a philosopher.

would reveal the inadequacy of their own straitened curriculum, and that the habits of reasoning thus cultivated would dethrone superstition *more geometrico*. Similarly, for the ascetic Hasidism of his day (but not for its later development), the *Autobiography* is a prime source.

Even for the student of the history of ideas, therefore, Maimon's principal work is his *Autobiography*. For the ordinary reader technical appraisal of his scientific work is almost irrelevant; the student will know where to turn for such things, for critical accounts of Jewish life in Prussia and Poland, or for a prosopography of personages alluded to. Here we need only mention the date of Maimon's birth, which was 1754; the date of the *Autobiography,* which was first published in 1792-93, and the date of his death, which was 1800. From the *Autobiography* itself the reader would infer that Maimon's patrons were all soon to desert him. Whether the patrons were more alienated by Maimon's intellectual arrogance and contempt for duller wits, his cadging and chicanery, his dissolute habits, or his heterodox beliefs, readers will decide according to their own hierarchy of values. They did forsake him, and he did drown himself in drink. When his former patrons washed their hands of him, he was given shelter on the estate of the youthful Count Adolf von Kalckreuth in Silesia, and there he philosophized and drank until he succumbed. It is a measure of the man's personal success, and oddly gratifying, if only for the perverse satisfaction that the probable discomfiture of the former patrons affords, to know that the ragged Talmud scholar from Poland managed to die in a German nobleman's castle as the nobleman's guest.

To achieve full spiritual freedom Maimon had deliberately to cut himself off from the Jewish as from the respectable community in general. What he had done when he had left the Polish ghetto and after having found a precarious welcome by Berlin's "enlightened" Jewry, he did all over again when he scandalized Mendelssohn and German-Jewish society. This left him apparently with but a single alternative—baptism and admission to Gentile respectable society. Maimon again refused. In renouncing, one after the other, Jewish ghetto life in the East, Jewish society in the West, and Gentile respectability, Maimon staked out the path that a succession of great Jews were to follow. Many of those who did most to enrich European culture and traditions were Bohemians who lived outside the limits of Jewish society and still refused to become members of any other well-defined community. Maimon was the first of them as Heinrich Heine probably was the greatest, who prophesied that at his death neither mass nor kaddish would be chanted.

Maimon's *sans souci,* however, was without a trace of the sarcastic or sentimental bitterness of his successors. He still possessed all the cheerfulness of the Enlightenment's confidence in reason, and if he nourished Ulysses' longing for Ithaca, it was for an Ithaca of the spirit—already impossible a few decades later, but not so hopeless at the turn of the nineteenth century.

In the preface to the first edition of the *Autobiography,* Karl Philipp Moritz (who deserves great credit for bringing it out) emphasizes its value not only for its description of the sad state of Jewish culture outside Germany, but particularly as a useful example of a successful struggle for knowledge in the face of insuperable obstacles. These merits none will gainsay; but perhaps we need now no longer pass over the rest of the book in apologetic silence—heterodoxy and roguery, if their stature is sufficient, may also qualify for admission to a gallery of worthies.

The present edition is based upon the translation of J. Clark Murray, Professor of Mental and Moral Philosophy at McGill College, Montreal, published in London in 1888.

The original German text, an extensive one, and burdened with many learned asides, has been here reduced to a clear and uninterrupted account of Maimon's extraordinary life.

MOSES HADAS